How the Church lost The Way . . .

. . . and how it can find it again

Steve Maltz

SAFFRON PLANET

Saffron Planet
PO Box 2215
Ilford IG1 9TR
UK
T: +44 (0)208 551 1719
E: contact@saffronplanet.net

First published 2009

ISBN 978-0-9562296-0-1

Cover design by Phil Maltz
Typeset by CRB Associates, Reepham, Norfolk
Printed in Malta

Contents

Part Three: Balance

Acknowledgements

My thanks and love to all the usual suspects. You know who you are and you are all too modest for a name-check. Couldn't do it without you, though.

Thank you, Holy Spirit, for filling up this empty shell with timely knowledge, contacts, and experiences and yet again bringing together all of those strands in such a marvellous way.

Foreword

The removal of stubborn grease requires drastic treatment! Simple cleaners may not do the trick: pretty strong stuff may be required to force the grease out.

"Greece" in the Church also needs removing! Few of us have much idea of the level of contamination that Greek thinking has produced in the Church through the ages. To say that drastic treatment may be required to remove it is an understatement. It is no exaggeration to say that ancient Greek ideas have bedevilled Christendom. Its legacy is twofold, producing on the one hand "Christians" that are so spiritually minded they have little impact on society; on the other, "Christians" that are so identified with the world that they have no real testimony at all.

Steve Maltz has beaten me to it! For many years I have wanted to write a book along these lines. But Steve has rendered us all a great service in exposing the trap of Greek thinking, showing us how to break free and return to Church life as Jesus wants it. Free of the crippling influence of Greek thinking and free to move in the fullness of Christ.

Read this book; enjoy this book; but above all, learn the lessons of this book. They are profoundly important for the successful testimony of the true Church in these end days.

Christopher Hill
Bible teacher and broadcaster

Introduction

It's a presumptuous title for a book, don't you think?

How the Church lost The Way . . .

It's a double whammy. There's a simple angle and a clever one.
Firstly, we can take it at face value and ask ourselves what has
gone wrong with the Church? Actually, this is not a biting
critique of the Church today. There are no crude frontal assaults
at the clerical edifices or cunning strikes at the soft underbelly
of the ecclesiastical world. It is merely an analysis of a series of
events that occurred in the far-off past, in the formative years
of the established Church. It is a reference to a process that
started many centuries ago and has continued unabated ever
since.

We can also look again at the title and see something else.
Before the Church had got used to calling itself *The Church*, it
was called *The Way*. So the implication here is that the Church
didn't just lose its way, but it lost touch with its origins. At some
point in its history it stopped being called *The Way*.

So what? It's just a name, isn't it? Well, it's a good name if you
think about it. It has an air of certainty and exclusivity. For a
central figure who claimed that He was not just The Way to God
but the *only* way, this alternative name for the fledgling Church
is a pretty good one. Yet once the events of the Book of Acts were
all played out, the name disappears from history. And so did the
certainty and the exclusivity of the message at the heart of it.

Now for the subtitle.

> *. . . and how it can find it again.*

To which, your reasonable response is . . .

Oh yes, what makes you so sure you have the answers, if indeed there is a problem to start with?

Here is the problem.

It's subtle, but it's there nonetheless. It was highlighted to me recently in a church that I was regularly attending. The memory verse for that year was to be Romans 1:16 and they proclaimed it on a card given out to church members. It read, *"I am not ashamed of the gospel, because it is the power of God for the salvation of everyone who believes . . . "*

Sounds right, but it's not the *whole* story. You see, they had missed out the last bit of the verse, *" . . . first for the Jew, then for the Gentiles"*. Also, in that same church, a sermon series in Romans skipped seamlessly from the end of Romans 8 to the start of Romans 12, as if the missing three chapters – the key New Testament chapters on the role and future of the Jews – inhabited some parallel universe!

You may deem me over-sensitive on this issue. After all, I am a Christian of Jewish birth and that would make me over-vigilant for any whiff of anti-Semitism. And this is true, but my concern is not for myself, or for fellow Jews, but for the Church itself.

Thumbing through what is described as one of the most widely used textbooks in Christian theology,[1] authored by one of the most respected theologians of our age, two observations surprised and shocked me. Firstly, in the extensive index, there was not a single reference for any of the following terms, *Jewish*, *Israel* or *Hebrew* (or *Hebraic*), whether as single words or within phrases. Secondly it was stated that the key debates in the early Church on Jesus Christ were conducted in Greek and in the light of the presuppositions of major Greek schools of philosophy.

To an impartial observer studying the Bible and subsequent Christian history, it would seem that a Jewish-based faith, defined by the Bible, had become a Greek philosophy, defined by arguments birthed in the minds of Socrates, Plato and their ilk. Yes, this is a very simplistic deduction, but gut feelings often uncover crude truths, that layers of sophistication, tradition and cleverness can sometimes mask. It is surely significant that the textbook index had as many references to Plato as the apostle Paul and for Aristotle just double the total and add some. But, as for Moses, just a big fat zero. What was it about these Greek philosophers and their influence on Christian thought? Did God use them to shed much needed extra light on our faith? Does that mean that the Bible is insufficient for our needs? Important questions, but seldom asked and rarely answered.

I have already stated that the perceived problem is a subtle one, but no way is it a trivial one. The scenarios outlined are just symptoms of a problem in the Church, a historical process that has been going on for centuries in most churches, whatever their denomination.

The process of stripping out every trace of Jewishness from the established Church started officially as a result of a decision made in the fourth century AD and has been motoring along quite nicely ever since. Yet it seems to be in direct opposition to one of the Apostle Paul's major declarations as to what the Church of Jesus Christ was to be, in his letter to the Ephesians:

> *"For he himself [Jesus] is our peace, who has made the two one [Jews and Gentiles] and has destroyed the barrier, the dividing wall of hostility, by abolishing in his flesh the law with its commandments and regulations. His purpose was to create in himself one new man out of the two, thus making peace, and in this one body to reconcile both of them to God through the cross, by which he put to death their hostility."*
> (Ephesians 2:14–16)

Speaking first in metaphor we see that God's purpose was that the Body of Christ should be a mixed-race man, part Jew, part Gentile. What this means is that the Church was always meant to have Jewish and Gentile elements. The fact that this has never really happened in history does not prove God wrong, it just paints the Church as unfulfilled. The Church was meant to be an entity with Jew and Gentile at peace and reconciled and no-one can ever claim that it has ever got even close to that ideal. But it doesn't mean that it is never going to happen because God's Word does not lie. It's going to happen and some people claim they know how it is going to happen. So are they right or are they wrong? We can only answer that once we find out what they are saying.

The "One New Man" movement that has recently appeared in the USA is to be commended in that it seeks to restore the Hebrew roots of Christianity, lost since the fourth century AD, when the established Church started its campaign of extermination of all things Jewish. But, just like a catherine wheel, going from a steady jerkiness to all out mayhem in a matter of seconds, some in the movement, after first taking it to a reasonable place, just let rip, confusing some Gentiles into believing that they had, in some way, become Jewish! It is acceptable to restore Jewishness where relevant, but not to the extent that there would be a blurring of identity and Gentiles would be seen worshipping in full Jewish garb, going to Yiddish classes and eating Kosher. This can't be right. Someone lit the fuse and the whole lot has gone all gefilte fish!

This has been something that has troubled me for many years. It is OK to bring back the Jewish elements, but surely God was speaking about a balance between Jew and Gentile? Surely folk could see that a mainly Jewish Church is no more the answer than the mainly Gentile Church that has been the status-quo for sixteen centuries. Isn't God talking about a balanced arrangement here? If He is, then there is some serious rethinking to be done.

As I sit in churches, I wonder how much that I see and hear would be different if Paul's "One New Man" declaration had caught on. Would there still be icons, statues and murals? Would there be churches and cathedrals as we know them, at all? Would the structures and hierarchies be any different? What about worship styles and liturgies? Then my mind wandered as it wondered. What about the catering? Would Alpha courses become Aleph courses? Will we all be singing choruses in Hebrew? Would the preacher need coaching in stand-up comedy?

My imagination was stirred. So I decided to investigate further.

Notes

1. *Christian Theology*, Alister McGrath, Blackwell Publishing 2007.

Prologue

We start with a mental exercise. Not an easy one, but a useful one and one that hopefully will prepare your mind for what it is about to receive. No, I am not proposing a New Age emptying of thoughts, but rather a realisation of what lies beneath them. Imagine you have just woken up to a new day. Then mentally trace through it, concentrating on your voluntary actions, rather than the more mundane (though serious) processes that actually keep your body alive. Here's what could be a typical day.

> Woke up, got out of bed, dragged a comb across my head, then realised I had just paid a homage to The Beatles. Ah, The Beatles. Memories flooded back of the previous night at the themed bar, guzzling too much food and beer, while being entertained by a rather good Beatles tribute band. Ah, The Beatles. The first worldwide celebrities of pop culture, trendsetters in music, fashion, drug taking, political agitation and communication. These hazy thoughts were swept aside by pangs of hunger and I had a full fry-up for breakfast, then went to work. Once there, I just counted the hours to clocking-off, mechanically going through the processes of my allotted tasks, but my mind focused on the football game I was going to later . . .

OK, so what? Given that I've just described a typical day for someone living in the West in the twenty-first century, there must be a purpose to the exercise. Before the great unveiling I will move to a Sunday and repeat the mental process, but focusing on the daily activities of a typical Christian.

Woke up, got out of bed, prayed and did my devotions. Slight dread but duty first, put on my "Sunday best", cleanse my mind of distractions, then Church. Sit there quietly, sing the songs, listen to the sermon, mind wandering . . . 4,000 holes in Blackburn Lancashire, what the? . . . walk to the altar, take communion, polite conversation, then leave the church, change clothes, then an afternoon in town, take in a show, some Chinese food, a few drinks. Home late at night, not looking forwards to work tomorrow, just need to get through the week until the next weekend. Get ready for bed, prayers and sleep.

Of course you may not connect with this entire list, but I guarantee there are at least some familiar aspects. Now to the big point, the climax, the denouement. If I told you that, in both lists, you are chiefly following processes flowing from the thoughts and practices of a civilisation that flourished in a land many miles eastward, many centuries ago. And that land was not the Middle East of Jesus, two thousand years ago, but rather the Greece of four hundred years or so earlier than the Christian era. And ideas flowing from that land of Greece are very much still alive and kicking. In fact they set the foundations and principles behind our daily lives in our modern world. Let that sink in for a few moments.

Look at people going about their daily lives. Some stride purposefully around, secure in their imagined immortality. They live guilt-free lives filled with pleasure. For a growing number, the working week has no other purpose than facilitating the wild excesses of the weekend. Others are not so secure. The certainties of old had been eroded, leaving behind a confusion of beliefs and philosophies. Some mix and match and hope for the best, others just retreat from the world, yet others reject everything save that which feeds their self-interests. Then there are those who just shrug their shoulders and get on with things. *What will be, will be*, they chant. Finally there are those who don't care any more and have given up.

There's nothing new under the sun. This same scenario was

a perfect fit just over two thousand years ago, in the streets of Ancient Greece. The difference is that each of the attitudes painted were, for them, schools of thought and philosophy. The names will be familiar to you. The *Epicurianists* took meaning from modest pleasures, while the *Hedonists* took this to the extreme. The *Eclectics* were the mix and matchers, while the *Ascectics* turned their back on the world and its pleasures. The *Sceptics* just rejected everything, while the *Cynics* took this further and just lived for themselves. The *Stoics* simply put it all down to fate while the *Nihilists* denied any sort of meaning at all.

We may be separated from these folk by two thousand years of Christianity but the cynics (I worked that one in quite cleverly, didn't I?) among us would wonder why our society, as a whole, seems to have rejected the certainties of the Gospel of Jesus and have slipped back into those ancient ways. To make matters worse, there are aspects of many of these philosophies in the Christian Church too. These and other Greek ideas are very much a part of the modern ecclesiastical world. So when was the Church infiltrated? When did we turn our backs and let these pagan ideas in?

The answer is simple, serious and startling and it's the subject of this book.

PART ONE
Wisdom

" . . . Greeks look for wisdom . . . "
(1 Corinthians 1:22)

A Tale of Two Summits – Part 1

Summits are rewards after a long arduous climb. They are also meetings of significance. There were two such summit meetings in the early days of the Church. The first represented a climb down by key delegates and the second represented a groundbreaking thrust into unfamiliar uncharted territories. Both had a huge impact on the fledgling Church as they addressed the question "where can we go next?" and we are still feeling the effects of where we did actually go next as a result of those meetings, held in Jerusalem in AD 49 and in Nicaea in AD 325.

There's a series of Christian cartoons for kids, where the modern-day heroes are transported back in time to Bible days and interact with real characters in familiar stories. With no consideration of the time paradoxes that have worried Trekkies and other sci-fi nerds in similar situations, these brave heroes would meet Noah and Jonah, watch the parting of the Red Sea and witness the nativity of Jesus. Why let the kiddies have all the fun, we are going to follow in this fine tradition, travelling back in time and witnessing, not the glamour and thrills of Bible adventures, but the goings-on at these two summit meetings. This idea may not fill you with much passion and excitement, but in terms of drama and significance, parish council meetings they weren't!

So, with the liberty of authors' license, without a Tardis or DeLorean car in sight, we travel back to Jerusalem, around twenty years since the crucifixion of Jesus . . .

The room was far too small for the number of men who had gathered there. It was large enough to sleep a small party of pilgrims at Passover. It was also large enough to accommodate that ragtag group a couple of decades earlier, who had sheltered there at Passover just after the untimely death of their leader, Jesus. Now, many of the same people were present at this summit meeting, convened by their leader, James. But as this number had virtually doubled, the room was decidedly *not* large enough for comfort and convenience. But these people were poor and lived at the very margins of society, so it wasn't simply a case of booking a conference hall or convention centre.

There were three groups of people crammed into this upper room. Half the room was full of elders and men with the air of leadership and importance. They were all facing the wide shallow window on the east side, through which the morning sun cast bright beams that framed a man who stood, facing the others. This was Peter, tall, thickset, his face a sculpture of determination. Huddled in the corner on floor cushions sat Paul and Barnabas, the heavyweight division, uncharacteristically quiet, following the protocol of observers. In the other corner were Thomas, Matthew and Philip, veteran disciples, original followers of Jesus. And between them all, a servant girl, Rhoda, a vision of perpetual motion, was twisting and turning, fetching drinks and baskets of food to and fro.

This meeting of Jewish believers in the risen Jesus had been convened to address one problem, "the Gentile problem". What to do with them? It was a lot neater when God was drawing believers just out of His ancient chosen people. After all, they had two thousand years of dealing with God, while the Gentiles were flailing about without law, direction or purpose. After all He was *their* God, wasn't He? OK, it hadn't been a strife-free relationship, but, don't forget, *they* were bearers of the marks of covenant, circumcision in the flesh. What can Gentiles know of the things of God?!

It had been a hard lesson, but God had made it absolutely clear to them, through Peter's episode with Cornelius the centurion, that the Gentiles did have a future in God's plan. Hadn't the prophet Isaiah declared, *"I have made you a light for the Gentiles, that you may bring salvation to the ends of the earth."* That wasn't the problem that had forced this summit meeting in Jerusalem. They were meeting to discuss practical matters. It wasn't *how could God extend His kingdom to the Gentiles*, but rather *how can Gentiles live out their new faith?*

The very things that had ensured the survival of the Jews through their two thousand year history were now to provide a stumbling block. The Jews were used to being a people separate. God had kept them apart from the nations that surrounded them, through stringent laws and customs, but most of all through the mark of circumcision, the unique branding that ensured that a Jew stayed a Jew and belonged to God, in body if not always in mind.

How could Gentiles be grafted into this whole *thing*? To some, such as the apostles Matthew, Thomas and Philip, it was clear. They would need to go through adult circumcision – it was the only way. This opinion had been voiced earlier in the Jerusalem meeting, despite a spirited report from Paul and Barnabas on their successes with the Gentiles, on their travels. Nevertheless, before Peter had been allowed to speak, a Pharisee had just argued his case. *"Without circumcision these Gentiles are lost!"* he asserted. *"And they must also follow Torah, just as we do"*, he added. Most seemed to be in agreement with this, but not Paul and Barnabas and certainly not Peter, who, after much private discussion, was now speaking.

> *"Brothers, you know that some time ago God made a choice among you that the Gentiles might hear from my lips the message of the gospel and believe."*

This had been around a dozen or so years earlier, when Peter had received his revelation at the house of Cornelius. This was old news by now for the delegates at the meeting, but, among the nods and casual shrugs, there were still some that, you can see, hadn't yet adjusted to this situation. Peter continued.

"God, who knows the heart, showed that he accepted them by giving the Holy Spirit to them, just as he did to us. He made no distinction between us and them, for he purified their hearts by faith."

He stopped and looked around, as if trawling for any hints of dissent. Before the slight murmurs had risen to a disruptive level, he resumed his speech.

"Now then, why do you try to test God by putting on the necks of the disciples a yoke that neither we nor our fathers have been able to bear? No! We believe it is through the grace of our Lord Jesus that we are saved, just as they are."

At that he sat down abruptly, momentarily startling those in front of him, who were now faced by the full beams of the rising sun. As if on cue, Paul and Barnabas stood up and shifted over to the position vacated. With much muttering and the occasional gasp or two, the delegates heard of the miraculous signs and wonders God had done among the Gentiles through them in Iconium and Lystra, such as the man who was crippled from birth, healed by just a command from Paul.

The meeting was drawing to a close and it was up to the leader of the Jerusalem church to sum up the proceedings. This was James, the half-brother of Jesus, who knew him better than any man still alive and had also met him once since his death, in a personal resurrection appearance. A highly respected leader and a righteous man, he was not known as *James the Just* for nothing. So when this stalwart of the Torah, this upstanding and outstanding individual stood up to make a judgement, people listened. He spoke.

> *"Brothers, listen to me. Simon has described to us how God at first showed his concern by taking from the Gentiles a people for himself. The words of the prophets are in agreement with this, as it is written:*
>
> > *'After this I will return*
> > *and rebuild David's fallen tent.*
> > *Its ruins I will rebuild,*
> > *and I will restore it,*
> > *that the remnant of men may seek the Lord,*
> > *and all the Gentiles who bear my name,*
> > *says the Lord, who does these things'*
> > *that have been known for ages.'"*

They continued to listen in silence, as the preamble gave way to proclamation.

> *"It is my judgment, therefore, that we should not make it difficult for the Gentiles who are turning to God. Instead we should write to them, telling them to abstain from food polluted by idols, from sexual immorality, from the meat of strangled animals and from blood. For Moses has been preached in every city from the earliest times and is read in the synagogues on every Sabbath."*

And so you witness perhaps the first really key decision of the early Church. *What was to be done about the Gentiles?* What James proposed was not just an arbitrary compromise on the spur of the moment, he had given some thought to this.

Some say that what James proposed for the Gentiles was a distillation of the basic laws God gave to Noah after the flood. Based on Genesis chapter 9 and expanded on in the Talmud (Sanhedrin 56a), these laws were: practising justice and abstaining from blasphemy, idolatry, adultery, bloodshed, robbery and eating flesh torn from a live animal. As these laws were given in ancient times before the rise of Abraham and his family, before there were any Jewish people around, they are said to be the basic laws for mankind. As Jews were subsequently given the Torah to live by, according to the rabbis these laws of Noah are said to be the eternal laws for Gentiles, even up to the current day. On the other hand some have said that these prohibitions were based on the acts that a Jew must die rather than commit, though this only accounts for the immorality and the (implied) shedding of blood. Still others think that all James was doing was providing a way for realistic fellowship between Jews and Gentiles, offering these suggestions just as pointers rather than fixed commands and emphasising a stricter morality than they were used to.

The summit meeting was over and a letter dispatched to the Gentiles, listing these instructions, not as holy writ but rather as recommendations, with the parting words, *"You would do well to avoid these things."* The Jewish leadership of the Church had now offered an open invitation to the Gentiles. *Jesus is for you, too. Now let's move forwards together.*

To summarise this first great council of the Christian Church, it is clear that they acted out of pure zeal for the Gospel. A practical solution had to be found for a problem that had arisen due to the sheer speed of growth of their message. God had made it clear that the Gospel was for *all* people and so a way had to be found to make this possible, within existing frameworks.

If they hadn't addressed this situation then the Church would have failed before it had even got going. By forcing circumcision and Jewish culture upon Gentile converts, most would have fallen away, weighed down by these imposed burdens. Christianity would have been strangled by its own Jewish roots. Eventually it would have been decimated by the pagans, as just another atheist (i.e. non-emperor worshipping) sect and would have become just a footnote in history. Perhaps it would have survived in some form, as a form of Rabbinic Judaism with added grace and salvation, but it is doubtful whether God would have looked down at it with favour. As for you Gentiles, you would have remained pagans, outside God's covenants, living lives of hedonism and lawlessness, guided by principles formulated by ancient Greek thinkers.

This leads quite nicely to the next episode in our journey, where we find out more about those ancient Greek thinkers. We ask the question, *how did they become so influential?* To answer this, we continue to travel back in time to the Greece of the fourth century BC.

God's Extended "Gap Year"

God created the world and saw that it was good. He then created men and women and gathered together a special people, the Jews, to work with. It wasn't plain sailing and for a few thousand years there was a love-hate contest unparalleled in history. He fed them, taught them, instructed them, blessed them and cursed them. In turn they listened, learned, worshipped, loved and rebelled. It was a stormy, fiery relationship that tried His patience exceedingly. Then, in 397 BC, He felt He needed a rest, packed His bags and went off on holiday for around four hundred years. It is what we Brits call a "gap year", when some take time off between school and college, to travel and either have a good time or indulge in worthy pursuits, depending on your inclination.

Not quite, of course. God is indefatigable and has no need for such distractions. The only time He rested was on the Sabbath in creation week, and that was purely to provide us with a working model of how we should live. Yet something undeniably happened in 397 BC, when the final words of the Old Testament were written, then the book closed, because what followed was a four hundred year silence from the heavens. Until He opened the new book of the New Testament and instructed the angel Gabriel to appear to Zechariah in the

Temple, there had been no universally accepted Holy Scripture, prophecy or divine visitations for four centuries.

But what *did* happen in this four century gap was very significant. It was as if the devil had seized the moment to act, taking God's apparent leave of absence as a licence to cause mischief. And, boy, did he give it some!

Let us focus on that year, 397 BC. Malachi was the last great prophet of ancient Israel. He spoke up for God. One last hurrah before the silence, one last chance for godly instruction, warning and correction. He spoke of the coming of Elijah the prophet, before that *great and dreadful day of the Lord*, but, unfortunately, no timetable was attached. It was to be a long wait, it still is!

In the meantime Artaxerxes II was ruling the mighty Persian Empire, the Romans were slowly building up their Republic, the Carthagians were suffering defeats, King An of Zhou was bossing China and, in Athens, Socrates, the first great philosopher of the modern age, was nearing the end of his controversial but influential life.

And this is where we go next because the spotlight in those "days of silence" switches from Israel to Greece. Around that time an awful lot of very clever and capable people had appeared on the scene, people who thought long and hard about the world around them and what made it tick. These were the philosophers and although they had already been around for a couple of centuries before this time, the stage had been prepared and set for the drama to come.

Socrates, take your bow. Enter stage left a pug-ugly little man in flowing robes. He stands there under the glare of the lights, blinking awkwardly but unbowed.

Socrates, why were you so significant?

You'll have to ask others. I couldn't possibly comment.

Enter stage right, Plato. Taller, younger, more dignified.

I'll speak up for Socrates. He is my teacher, my inspiration. In fact all my early work features the man himself in dialogue with others . . .

Socrates bows briefly and allows Plato to speak up for him . . .

Before my learned teacher entered the scene, we philosophers concerned ourselves with the world around us. Is the world made up of earth, air, fire and water, or are there smaller building blocks? Does mathematics govern everything? What about poetry? Socrates changed all that. What he taught us is to look within, at our moral beings, at what makes us tick . . .

Socrates was indeed influential, even for modern-day thinkers. So key was he that all who preceded him were lumped together in a single classification, the "Presocratics", the string of warm-up acts, preparing the audience for the main performer.

Socrates was a familiar figure in the streets of Athens. He was an effective teacher, his classrooms mainly the public spaces, his pupils taken from the rich young men of his day, with time on their hands and rebellion in their hearts. He taught them logic and the ability to reason. On the positive side one effect of this teaching was the jettisoning of the sorry, pathetic and argumentative bunch of Greek gods that had held sway for so long. Not so positive for him was that he was condemned to death by a repressive city government for "corrupting the young" and, most tellingly, "neglecting the gods".

Plato was Socrates' disciple. He was his biographer and recorded his ideas and became, in his own right, perhaps the most influential of all Socrates' pupils. He founded a school in Akademia, a suburb of Athens, the very first "academy". There people were instructed in mathematics, geometry, law and the natural sciences, as well as philosophy. He also wrote much. Much of his early writings were expanding on the ideas of Socrates, who wrote no books himself.

Plato never realised it, but his ideas were to become almost as influential as Jesus in the development of Western Christianity. There, I've said it, *perhaps the most controversial statement in this book.* Now all I have to do is prove it! He said a lot of stuff, wrote an awful lot of stuff, but it's his *one big idea* that we are going to focus on because this was to become a tiny seed that somehow got into the fertile soil of early Christianity and grew and grew until . . . you'll have to wait and see!

His one big idea was *the Theory of Forms*. Here's the story . . .

We tend to label these clever Greek thinkers as cerebral giants, masters of thought and reason and defenders of human logic. We expect them to think through all matters of the inner world of the mind and body in terms of the natural world, of just what can be seen, heard and perceived by the senses. Actually, that isn't true for this man. Plato was a man of ideas, but thought little of the world that surrounded him. He believed that there were two worlds, the obvious one that we live in and a "perfect" one, *somewhere else in the Universe*. I suppose this would be his concept of heaven and in this heaven exists what Plato called *Forms*.

To understand what these are, we need to think about everything that we see around us in our world, from actual objects like chairs and diamonds, to geometric shapes like squares and triangles, to concepts like beauty and goodness. Now you must realise that, according to Plato, all of these things are just imperfect copies of perfect chairs, diamonds, squares, triangles, beauty and goodness, that exist in the other "perfect" world. These items of perfection are Plato's *Forms*. Get your (imperfect) head around that, then!

Plato also believed that whereas most of us will never get to see these Forms, some of us would. These are the *guardians*, specially gifted and trained individuals, the philosophers of course! Plato explained all of this in his analogy of the cave.

Our lives are as prisoners deep inside a cave, where all we can see of objects are their shadows, projected on the wall by a fire. We believe that what we see is reality but we are mistaken. To see reality we have to leave the cave and see things as they really are, though most are content at just seeing the shadow shapes inside the cave.

According to Plato, the one who makes this step to leave the cave is the *guardian*, who is rewarded by viewing the "higher

Good", the source of all truth and reason. Here's an idea that seems vaguely Christian, so perhaps here's the first clue as to how on earth this idea managed to find a home in the early development of Christian thought.

This "higher Good" is the ultimate Form, top of the Forms, Plato's concept of God, though not the personal God as we know Him. This "higher Good" is what we must aspire to. This "higher Good" is an eternal reality that exists in a higher realm and our physical senses are just not equipped enough to see any more than a pale reflection. Plato likens this concept to the sun in two ways. Both cause things to exist and grow and both are sources of light. As it is light which enables our eyes to have a partial sight of reality, then "the higher Good" enables our minds to have partial knowledge of what is real.

So there is space for the concept of God, albeit an *impersonal* one, in Plato's philosophy. Plato's God does not answer prayers, or comfort those in distress, or teach his people or listen to the cries of the heart. Plato's God is most assuredly *not* our Father in Heaven.

Plato believed that there are absolute standards for such things as goodness, morality and truth, each of these existing as a perfect Form in this "second" world. He also believed in the eternal soul. So what's the problem with Plato? Well it all now starts to go downhill.

Plato believed that we are body and soul. He thought that these were totally separate entities, bound together temporarily during a person's lifetime. This was the concept of the *duality* of man. But, to Plato, the soul was the dominant, superior entity and it is immortal, being reborn again and again in different bodies, gaining in knowledge as it does so, like the concept of re-incarnation in Eastern religions. The soul is our seat of thought and knowledge, associated with the "second" perfect world. The body interacts through the five senses with our *imperfect* world and, to Plato, restricts the soul from attaining its full potential. So, in his view, the soul is good and the body is bad. Everything associated with the soul is good, everything associated with the body is bad. Fix this in your brain, it's the *Big Consequence* of Plato's "Big Idea".

Plato's Big Consequence: Soul = Good, Body = Bad

The third member of our influential team of Greeks is Aristotle, a pupil of Plato, the pupil of Socrates. The Greek equivalent of our Abraham, Isaac and Jacob may not have been linked by a bloodline, but their ideas form the foundation of Western thought. But Aristotle does not follow the party line, he has new things to teach us. If you were to summarise the main difference it would be that, whereas Plato was poetical and mystical, Aristotle was very much more practical and earthy in his approach.

Whereas Plato took this airy-fairy "second" world of Forms as his starting point, Aristotle was more interested in our world. He was an avid collector and classifier. His brain roamed freely, covering a wide breadth of subjects and was said to be the first to create a system of Western philosophy that included just about everything, from morality and logic to science and politics. His scientific work in the area of natural history, relying on observation of the real world, led to Charles Darwin acknowledging him as the first biologist. In some four hundred books, he laid foundations in astronomy, physics and chemistry and provided a bridge between the disciplines of physics and philosophy in creating "metaphysics", which examines such basic questions as the nature of being and knowing. An urban legend among historians claims that Aristotle was the ultimate know-it-all, probably the last person who actually knew everything there was possible to know in the society in which he lived.

Yes, that's all very well, but what was his "Big Idea"? Well, there was one discovery of his that helped shape the world and is still with us now. This is what we call *logic*, or rather *deductive* logic. Yes someone had to discover it, it didn't just drop out of the sky, it is an actual discipline and Aristotle laid down all the groundwork. He gave himself the task of thinking logically about every aspect of human life.

He introduced the *syllogism*, which uses deduction to lead from two premises to a conclusion. Here's how that works. Our first premise is that all blackbirds can fly. Our second premise is "here is a blackbird" (imagine you are looking at a picture of one). From these two statements the conclusion is that this particular blackbird can fly. It seems obvious to us, but perhaps not before Aristotle came along. Aristotle did so much work in the area of human thought and logic that his ideas became the very vocabulary of Western thought, even in the Church that wasn't to arrive until hundreds of years after his death. In that way his influence is subtle and hard to understand, but understand it we must at least try to do! This we will come back to in the next chapter, but for now we will accept Aristotle's "Big Idea" as his use of logic in understanding the world. And the consequence of Aristotle's "Big Idea"?

Aristotle's Big Consequence: Everything can be determined through logic and the senses.

Aristotle is not going to figure much in our story, as Plato is very much the major influence on the development of the early Church and, as we shall see, his ideas are the ones that ultimately did the most damage! You can imagine the movie titles. *The Church and Plato – the Infant Years* and *The Church and Aristotle – the Adolescent Years*.

To summarise then, in the four centuries between the closing of the Old Testament and the opening of the New Testament, God's extended "Gap Year", a whole flood of new ideas and new ideals was pouring out of Greece. You may now start to see the relevance of this, because these ideas and ideals were not going to just impact the world, but the Church too. In the Apostolic Palace in the Vatican is a painting by Raphael. It is known as *The School of Athens* and features a whole gaggle of

Greek philosophers. Clearly seen are Plato and Aristotle in conversation. Plato is pointing above to the heavens and Aristotle is pointing down to the earth. This sort of sums up their differing views but the question we need to ask is why they should be commemorated in the capital of the Roman Catholic Church?

In fact the Church is going to be well and truly infiltrated by the teachings of Plato and Aristotle, as we shall see in the next chapter.

Beware Greeks Bearing Gifts

So where are we in our story? We have already covered two key developments in the history of mankind, the rise of Greek philosophy and the birth of the Christian Church. Now sit back and listen to the story of how they came together. Hold onto your seats, it may not be a pretty sight.

The Church as we know it today didn't just pop up out of nowhere. It is today's snapshot of a continuous historical process that started effectively when the Holy Spirit descended on that small group in Jerusalem a few weeks after the Resurrection.

For a body whose chief mandate is to gather people of all backgrounds and cultures into its fold, staying pure and unsullied while it focused on its received mission was always going to be an issue. Contrast this with Israel in Old Testament times. Their mandate *was* to stay pure and holy, by living a separate existence from the world that surrounded them. By living within a wall of regulations, the *Torah* given by God to Moses, Israel was equipped to remain unsullied by the pagan nations around them.

Yet ultimately they failed, seduced by rival gods and prostituting themselves to alien lifestyles and were reprimanded by God as a result. But their failure was not a total one, thank goodness. The messianic bloodline was protected and Jesus arrived in the world as a member of the Jewish community, albeit one under foreign occupation and the salvation story was allowed to unfold.

The point being made here was that a nation socially engineered by God Himself to remain pure and untouched by alien ideas, fails to remain so, thanks to the basic restlessness of the human heart (rather than any fault of God's). How much more so will another group, the early Christians, whose very *raison d'être* is to "reach the world", become tainted in turn by the very people it is trying to reach?

This tainting began fairly soon after that Council in Jerusalem of Acts 15. Paul himself acknowledged that other worldviews would need to be addressed, just two chapters later.

> *"Paul then stood up in the meeting of the Areopagus and said: 'Men of Athens! I see that in every way you are very religious. For as I walked around and looked carefully at your objects of worship, I even found an altar with this inscription:* TO AN UNKNOWN GOD. *Now what you worship as something unknown I am going to proclaim to you. The God who made the world and everything in it is the Lord of heaven and earth and does not live in temples built by hands. And he is not served by human hands, as if he needed anything, because he himself gives all men life and breath and everything else. From one man he made every nation of men, that they should inhabit the whole earth; and he determined the times set for them and the exact places where they should live. God did this so that men would seek him and perhaps reach out for him and find him, though he is not far from each one of us. "For in him we live and move and have our being." As some of your own poets have said, "We are his offspring."'"*
> (Acts 17:22–28)

This meeting place is also translated as "Mars Hill". It is interesting to note that this is the name currently adopted by two key churches in the USA that are attempting to interface with the culture of the day, albeit in different ways. This is what Paul was doing in Acts 17, but little did he know that, within a century, the floodgates would have been opened and the Hebrew faith in Jesus the Messiah was going to be thoroughly swamped by the Greek culture of the day.

It all started with Plato. He was so key to everything that, in the twentieth century, the philosopher A. N. Whitehead suggested that all of Western philosophy ultimately consists of no more than *footnotes* to Plato. But it's the Church we're interested in, so what happened there?

Plato founded a seat of learning in Athens called the *Academy*, which continued after he died, ensuring that his philosophy, *Platonism*, flourished. When Christianity spread westwards from Jerusalem to the lands to the east of the Mediterranean, it was Platonism that was encountered first. The early Church fathers had to make a decision. *Do we ignore the prevailing culture, engage with it or learn from it?*

It seems that engagement, as with Paul in the Areopagus, was the best way forwards, yet the Church Fathers took it a lot further than that. Trained in Greek thought, they saw no danger in constructing a Christian worldview in the light of the teachings of Plato. One of these teachers, Justin Martyr, had the view that Platonists would be so challenged by the similarities between their worldview and Christianity, that they may consider conversion. It seems that what may have started as engagement for the purposes of evangelism, swiftly gave way to debate, then compromise, then finally assimilation. Christianity could have been said to have become a subdivision of Platonism with added grace!

So how could this have happened? It all started with the Jews, strangely enough, or one in particular. Philo was his name and he lived in Alexandria in Egypt, one of the most famous cities in the world at that time. It was just after the time of Jesus.

Philo may have been a Jew but his education was thoroughly Greek, in common with all Jews living in the Egyptian capital. Yet he was a loyal and proud Jew and his life's ambition was to bring together his religious heritage and his philosophic tendencies. He believed he saw continuity between Moses and Plato.

The problem of his day was that many Jews, trained in Greek ways, were rejecting Moses and the Bible and so Philo worked hard to create a compromise that would be acceptable. His main work was in the creation of Bible commentaries, mainly of the Book of Genesis, and he was the first to do so with one finger figuratively in the pages of the Bible and the other in the life and works of Plato.

We can start at the Creation story. To Plato (and to Philo), the Universe came into being through the work of the *Demiurge*, not quite God as we know Him, but a lesser god. Remember Plato's Big Consequence, that the soul is good, the body is bad, the concept of *dualism*. This can be simplified further in saying that anything of the physical world is *inferior* to anything of the spiritual world. So this Demiurge, responsible for the Creation of the physical Universe, just has to be an inferior god, from Plato's point of view.

The concept of the Demiurge is a consequence of Platonism. It is a fudge to support a faulty philosophy. That is the problem if your starting point is a falsehood. Everything that follows from it is also false and you're just sinking further and further into the mire. This is even the case with techniques used to implement your ideas. The technique that Philo used most of all when he turned to the Books of Moses is the same one already used in the study of Greek texts, such as those of Homer. This tool is known as *allegory* and the damage it did to the biblical text is incalculable.

Allegory. In the context of this book it's a key concept, so it's worth labouring the point in order to fully understand it in every way. It is defined as a way of representing a situation, giving it a meaning that is not a literal meaning. Examples are the best way of getting a grip of this:

George Orwell's *Animal Farm* is an allegory of the Soviet era of Stalin in the pre-war years. Whereas kids may have a hate figure in Napoleon the pig, there is a greater hate figure implied as Stalin himself. So, if we take the story *literally*, it's just a story of talking animals on a farm, but *allegorically* it's a political satire.

The movie *The Wizard of Oz*, gave a lot of joy to generations of kids, with its basic homespun philosophy. It also exercised the brains of generations of scholars and commentators who saw allegory all over the place in it. So, in its literal sense, it's just a good kid's yarn, but as an allegory it is mostly seen by economists as a critique of the gold standard (no time here to explain that one!)

One big question we need to ask is whether the author intended to create an allegory and, if so, what point is he making? In George Orwell's case, the allegory was clear and unambiguous. With The Wizard of Oz, L. Frank Baum, the author, never made it clear what the real meaning of the movie was.

So what about the Bible? Well, we know the author, God Himself. So when Philo went through the text of the early books of the Old Testament, he had to be sure that, if he saw allegory, then the author Himself would need to be in agreement. And, if He wasn't, then Philo was treading on dangerous ground indeed!

Why would Philo have to use allegory anyway and what's this to do with Plato? Well, it's back to Plato's "Big Idea", his *dualism*, and it's worth delving deeper to extract the core thinking behind it. When Plato says that the soul is good and the body is bad, he is declaring a basic principle that has many guises. In religious terms, he is saying that the physical world, the one in which we live, is bad (or evil) and the spiritual world (heaven and such places) is good, and therefore worth striving for. So, material world is bad . . . spiritual world is good. This theme is going to pop up again and again in this book, as you begin to realise how deep this idea has sunk into our collective minds.

Because of this, Philo was uncomfortable whenever, in the Bible, God (a spiritual being) mixes it with us on a human level (the material world), when He interacts with man personally, or shows human characteristics or emotions. You would expect that he would have had a real problem with Jesus – their lifetimes actually overlapped. Perhaps they actually met each other? When Philo wrote of such God-man interactions in his Bible commentaries, he would look beyond any literal interpretations of the verse for deeper meanings, *allegories*. In fact this became a regular feature of his work, looking for deeper "spiritual" meanings behind Bible verses that the author (God) meant just to be taken literally. Often he accepted that Bible verses could have both a literal and an allegorical meaning.

In our story, Philo is but a stepping stone, so, rather than dwelling on him any further, we will move on a century or so to the next major figure of our story, Origen. He was a Christian, one of the *Church Fathers* and he, too, lived in Alexandria. In common with Philo, he had a passion for interpreting the Bible but there was a major difference here. Although Philo looked to marry the orthodox Jewish interpretations with insights that he believed that he had from Greek philosophy, he always saw himself as a Jew first and his writings always reflected that fact. Origen was a Gentile Christian who was writing Bible commentaries for other Christians in the Greek speaking world. For him, the Hebrew text and Jewish themes were just the raw data, to be processed using the tools of Greek understanding.

Origen was greatly influenced by both Philo and Plato but, in his approach to the biblical texts, went a stage further than Philo. Whereas Philo often gave literal and allegorical interpretations of the Scriptures, Origen tended to dwell on allegory. As a Christian heavily influenced by Plato, he saw the spiritual dimension as all-important, so strained to find "deeper" meanings wherever he could. In fact Origen was responsible for making allegory the dominant form of Bible interpretation for centuries to come.

A favourite theme of his was to re-interpret the Old Testament in the light of the New Testament, using techniques from Greek philosophy, married with insights from early Christian tradition and other writings. His driving principle was that the Bible contained three levels of meaning, corresponding to the body, soul and spirit. You can see the influence of Plato here, particularly when he adds that the "body" level of meaning, the literal meaning of the text, is for the more simple minded whereas the "soul" and more particularly the "spirit" levels of meaning are for the *more enlightened* readers. If Origen discerned where a Bible passage spoke about Christ, then, for him, this *had to be* the original meaning of the text. This may have come from the noblest of motives, but is it correct, is this what God had in mind when He authored the text?

Our next port of call of this whistle-stop tour of early Christian influences takes us to a place in the same African continent, two centuries later, to a place called Hippo, in modern day Algeria. We are going to meet the man who can be described in two different ways, depending on your perspective. To both the Catholics and Protestant reformers he is one of the most important figures in the development of Western Christianity. To others he is the philosopher who infused Christian doctrine with Platonism (or *Neoplatonism* to be specific). Like many of these Church Fathers, he was, by virtue of the sum of his influences, a *Christian philosopher*, a term that should by rights be an oxymoron.

Augustine of Hippo was enormously influential in many ways. From him we get the idea of original sin and our traditional understanding of evil. He has contributed much yet it is worth looking at what influenced him. He was originally a follower of *Manicheanism*, a cult that promoted a form of dualism, with good versus evil, light versus darkness, body versus soul. It was said to be a set of beliefs closer to Buddhism than Christianity.

His later influence was Ambrose, the Bishop of Milan, who introduced him to the Bible interpretation techniques of Philo and Origen. The fact is that Augustine was just so influential in the subsequent development of the Western Church, that if we perceive any issues in the way he interpreted the Bible, then this is going to have great consequences. So his take on such matters as "allegory versus literal readings of Scripture" is crucial.

Suffice to say that he follows in the tradition started by Philo and refined by Origen, in using Platonic techniques to interpret Bible texts. Although Augustine was correct in declaring that Scriptures are inspired of God, he reinforced Origen's ideas that Christ needs to be shoe-horned all over the Old Testament, even where the fit is uncomfortable and that allegorical interpretations were given to passages he was unsure of or unhappy with. His approach was to say that, in the first instance, readers must look at the spirit *behind* the literal texts, to grasp the mind of God, through *spiritual* understandings.

The scene has now been firmly established that, because of the demands of the Platonic world view in preferring the spiritual over the material, spiritual meanings were sought, even in Bible passages that were so obviously meant to be taken literally. A free-for-all was now created, allowing Christian teachers right up to the current day to be able to bend and coax God's Word to say whatever they want it to say!

All good things come to an end, more so bad things and the decline and fall of the Roman Empire is well documented, as is the subsequent rise of the Dark Ages. During this time much of the ancient wisdom of the Greeks was lost to the world and Aristotle in particular was forgotten. On the world stage Christianity gave way to Islam and two Arab scholars, Avicenna and Averroes, rediscovered the works of Aristotle. These teachings were eventually translated from Arabic into Latin and Christian Europe went crazy over this rediscovered philosopher. Posthumous appreciation of Aristotle reached Elvis-like proportions as Christian thinkers began to ask what this Greek philosopher could offer the Church. One man in particular put on his thinking cap and, undoubtedly, altered the course of Christian history.

This man was Thomas Aquinas, the last in our cast list of significant thinkers. A gentle giant, he was a Dominican monk living in the thirteenth century. To Aquinas, Aristotle was "the Philosopher" and he turned his huge brain to see what Aristotle could offer the world of Christian theology. His endeavours in marrying up the ideas of Plato, by way of Augustine and Aristotle, were so influential that he is considered by many Catholics as their greatest theologian and philosopher.

So, in a nutshell, what is a summary of Aquinas's teachings? In common with Aristotle, he was keen on using the rational mind and the senses, alongside his God-given faith. His ideas are explained in his greatest work, *Summa Theologica*. This is a guide to all the main theological teachings for the Catholic Church. It's rather large and complex but a good way to highlight the influence of Aristotle is to concentrate on just one aspect, that of the *sacraments*.

Before Aquinas came along, the seven sacraments – baptism, confirmation, reconciliation, the anointing, the Eucharist, holy orders and marriage – were seen as means of grace, ways by which God can bless individuals. Aristotle's influence, through Aquinas, was to modify this understanding into something more concrete. The best way for us to see the ideas of Aristotle in action is to look at the process of *transubstantiation*.

This is the Catholic belief that, as part of the Eucharist, Holy Communion, the bread and wine *actually* change into the body and blood of Christ on the altar. This indeed is a strange one. Jesus Christ present, in person, rather than just being present *symbolically*?

Aristotle taught that there is more to matter than its appearance. Every object also has *substance*, a kind of inner quality which defines it. An example given is that when water freezes it takes on a different appearance (ice), but is still the same substance (H_2O). Given this Greek understanding, Aquinas said that at the point of consecration at Holy Communion, although their appearance doesn't change, the *substance* of the bread and wine does, miraculously changing into the body and blood of Christ. This fact is accepted *by faith* by Catholics, despite the fact that the concept is fundamentally pagan.

So the whistle stop tour has ended. There has only been space to give you just a sketch of the issues raised by the infiltration of Greek philosophy into Christian theology. The ideas of Plato, refined by Philo (for a Jewish audience) and Origen (for a Christian audience), became thoroughly entwined with God's revelation to us, thanks to Augustine, the father of the Western Church. Then to this mix was added the ideas of Aristotle – despite being at odds with Plato on so many issues – and all put together by Thomas Aquinas, in the *Summa Theologica*, the most authoritative Catholic manual of theology.

As the next chapter is going to show, this hybrid of faith and reason was to prove most troublesome right from the early days of the Church.

A Tale of Two Summits – Part 2

If we had the answers to all of life's mysteries, then they wouldn't be mysteries any more and there would be less arguing among the experts. But, even among those of us who profess faith in an Almighty God who leads us into all truths, there are disagreements about all sorts of things. People have died over matters of Bible interpretation. Families have been split apart over obscure theological points. Religious differences are rarely trivial spats.

Did you know that the established Church split into two in the eleventh century, seemingly over the issue of a single word! The word was *filioque*, a Latin word translated as "and from the son". It was added to the original Creed by the Roman Catholics, but rejected by the Eastern Orthodox. The Orthodox believed that the Holy Spirit proceeds from the Father (God), whereas the Catholics believed that the Holy Spirit proceeded from the Father . . . *and the son* (Jesus). Although there were also political considerations involved here, regarding the location of the "Capital" of the Church, these disagreements were sufficient to destroy any hope of a unified world Church and led to the Eastern and Western Churches doing their own thing for the next thousand years. Can you believe it! We must ask ourselves, what was the real issue and why was it so important that unity had to be sacrificed to satisfy the protagonists?

The real issue seemed to be that the great doctrines of Christianity had become a philosopher's playground, a global forum for ideas and developments. These people loved to argue and the issue of the *filioque* had absolutely nothing to do with the Bible, but everything to do with the various ways the *Christian philosophers* interpreted the works of Plato. If he had only known the trouble he was going to bring, how his words, deployed within the context of pagan philosophy, were powerful enough to split the worldwide Christian Church!

Jews loved to argue too, though they had good reason. When your Holy Scripture is presented to you as words without vowels or punctuation, as it was with the Old Testament, one would expect the odd confusion or difference in opinion. These were conducted in the *yeshivas*, the places of study, and later on the pages of the *Talmud*, the written collection of rabbinic discussions. Lives were never threatened. There may have been spirited discussions, but it was all very civilized, blood was never spilt and, of course, it was always the interpretation of Holy Scripture that was argued over. Wrestling over the words of God to extract divine meanings somehow seems a nobler practice than arguing over points of philosophy that can never be resolved.

So when there are disagreements, particularly in matters of Bible interpretation, it is good to first look at the protagonists, to see what makes them tick, to check for unspoken agendas. For example it is rare to find an atheist arguing in favour of creationism or intelligent design. Having already decided on the non-existence of God, they must construct a world view that does away with any divine component. Therefore they will hold on to their beliefs in the theories of Darwinism, even when evidence doesn't fit, because the alternative is unthinkable. If evidence was presented that seemed to speak of the existence of God, would you expect them, in the true spirit of scientific enquiry, to rethink their position? No, because they have an agenda.

There is not a chance (notwithstanding a miraculous inter-vention of course) that they would compromise their agenda, because every agenda has an underlying cause, a *root*. In this example the root could be a number of things. It could be nurture (inherited atheism), it could be nature (a rational mind). It could be a fierce independence, not wanting to be accountable to a higher power. It could be a matter of lifestyle, leading to an aversion to any kind of moral code. Or it could be a cocktail of all or some of these possibilities.

It's the root we should examine, not the agenda that flows from it. Of course I have an agenda in writing this book. My agenda is to restore the understanding of the Hebraic roots of Christianity that has been lost, since the early days of the Church. But the root of my agenda is the fact that I was born a Jew. Not every Jewish Christian would share my agenda, many have been absorbed into the Church without any thought of their origins. That is fine, there is nothing wrong in that. In my case there is the matter of a calling to use my particular root to follow an agenda that I believe God has ordained for me. I hope that is clear, but it works for me.

All Christians have a shared agenda. We all believe in what Jesus has done for us and the teachings that we must follow as a consequence. Others may analyse us in other ways, just as I analysed the agenda of an atheist. They could also bring up nature (a character flaw) and nurture (inherited beliefs). Some may say that we are weak individuals in need of a crutch or an authority figure, others just think we are mad or deluded. In every case, as we well know, the real root of our agenda is the work of the Spirit of God in our lives, to convict us and sanctify us.

But there can be other agendas in the Body of Christ, let's call them *secondary* agendas. The path dictated by my Jewish roots became my agenda. Others follow different paths and agendas because we all have different roots. Your family could be lifelong Methodists, Anglicans, Baptists or Catholics (or any one of hundreds of others) and, through your formative years you would have taken on board many of their teachings and customs. You could have a Muslim, Jewish or Hindu background and, as in my case, this could help direct your path, perhaps equipping you as a missionary to your own people. Then there is the matter of your lifestyle or personal philosophy before your conversion. You could have lived a hedonistic lifestyle of debauchery and self-fulfilment. You could have been a communist, a conservative, a green activist, a vegetarian, an animal liberationist, a feminist, a homosexual, even an atheist. You may have been a naturally spiritual person, or a rationalist, even the hardened sceptic. These are our roots. Even before God comes into our lives, we all still have a set of beliefs, even if it is just a self-belief.

Then God hits us with the gospel, opens up our minds and hearts and leads us into an incredible adventure as a New Creation. His intention, I believe, is to take the raw material and mould us into something new and wonderful. In some cases, the Master Potter uses some old clay, parts of our "old creation", as He re-constructs us from inside out. But we are not inanimate objects, lifeless jars of clay, but are allowed to retain that most precious of gifts, our free will. By ensuring that we continue to act as individuals within the great worldwide network of the Body of Christ, it also opens us up to a danger. It is the temptation of individualism, perhaps allowing too much of our past lives to season our present and future lives. In these cases the root could act as a catalyst for disruption. It's a possibility and sometimes we need others to tell us if this is so.

My root of Jewishness could have led me to a form of legalism, an over-emphasis on striving to follow rules and regulations to such an extent as to stifle the Spirit that works within. Someone converted from a Muslim background could also have inherited a form of legalism from the rigid Shariah teachings of his past life. An ex-Hindu may have inherited a belief in multiple gods that has not yet been dealt with. An ex-communist may still be touched by humanism or may tend towards the contentious teachings of liberation theology.

And this all leads me to my main point, one of the key points in this book. There is a shared root by all who have lived and grown up in Western society. The root is the influence of the philosophies of Ancient Greece, which are far more prevalent than you could ever imagine. To try to understand this we are going on our second trip in time. Our first was to Jerusalem at the time of the Book of Acts, to that historic Council that paved the way for Gentiles to enter the Church. This second trip is to a place called Nicaea nearly four centuries later. A summit meeting is being held. It is the Council of Nicaea, in Turkey, in AD 325.

It was the fourth century's equivalent of a conference centre, but without the water coolers, wireless internet and pillow menu. It was, in fact, the imperial palace. By today's standards it was quite spartan, but none of the three hundred or so bishops who attended were complaining, there were more important issues to deal with than personal comfort.

This was the first great meeting of the wider Christian Church, though only around a sixth of the invitees actually became attendees. Delegates had come from far and wide, though only five came from the Western Church, and none from the land of Britain. And none of them were of Jewish descent. How things had changed since that earlier summit in Jerusalem!

You peer at the proceedings from behind an ornate pillar. Delegates are arranged in a semicircle, facing a raised dais, where two men sit on the left and right on jewel-encrusted thrones and a third stands dead centre behind a wooden lectern. Sitting on the right is the Patriarch, Alexander of Alexandria, chairman of the conference. The man on the left is the Emperor, Constantine, who had called the conference. He had already ensured that his throne was just that bit higher than the Patriarch's and, wearing a haughty expression, he sits impassively, seemingly bored with the proceedings.

Constantine. This man had a lot to answer for and, in terms of legacy, did almost as much damage as Plato, Origen and the rest of them. But, in the case of Constantine, there was no honour or altruism in his motives. The only good news about this Roman Emperor is that he put to an end the bloody persecutions of his predecessor, Diocletian. It seemed that the Church's worst enemy gave way to the Church's greatest friend. It must have seemed that way at the time, but the evidence of history showed that whereas Diocletian destroyed bodies, Constantine's decisions were to affect the soul of millions who came after him.

So who was he? Constantine was a military Emperor who worshipped the sun god and relied on this deity for success in battles. The key moment in his life happened on a bridge over a river. It was AD 312 and he was preparing for yet another skirmish when supposedly he had a vision of a cross against the sun, accompanied by the words, "In this sign, conquer". He took this to mean that his army should march into battle under the sign of the cross. It was all a bit vague and historians disagree about the actual chain of events, but the outcome was victory and the result was that *Christianity*, the religion of the Cross, was to become the state religion of the Roman Empire.

Meanwhile, in the imperial palace, Nicaea, the man at the centre of the stage, clutching the lectern, is Athanasius. He is speaking.

And so, bishops, I may be just a lowly deacon but I cannot but emphasise the importance of the decision we are going to make today.

He pauses for affect, looking around, but concentrates his gaze on the two dissenters, Secundus and Theonus, followers of Arius, who are seated directly in front of him. He continues.

The teachings of Arius must not be allowed to pollute the Holy Church. I will repeat my position, so perhaps those of you still suffering under delusion will come to your senses . . . Jesus Christ, the Son of God is of the same substance, homoousian with God the Father.

Any other position relegates our Lord to a mere creation, an unaccept-
able position.

The whole debate, pitting Arius against Athanasius, both of Alexandria, was indeed a crucial one. It was a debate created, argued and resolved with the language and ideas of Greek philosophy. Athanasius, and the majority of the bishops, believed in the *homoousian* position. Arius (naturally) took the arian position, which relegated Jesus to a created being. A third group took the compromised *homoiousian* position, where Jesus was *like* the Father. A contemporary called Basil sneered at this fudge, saying "that which is like can never be the same as that to which it is like". There were also the *homoian* and *heterousian* positions, but let's not go there!

It was both mind-stretching and mind-numbing but, to the Christian world as it was then, it was important and the deliberations at the Council of Nicaea were to produce the *Nicene Creed*, used to this day to remind us what we believe in and exactly who God, Jesus and the Holy Spirit are and what is their relationship with each other.

There was another issue discussed at this Council. It was deemed so important that Emperor Constantine himself took a leading role in the discussion. It concerned the timing of Easter. Because of the growing animosity towards the Jews, there were movements seeking to strip away all connection between this festival and the Jewish festival of Passover, where it owes its origins. Constantine is now reading the letter that he was going to circulate to churches throughout the Christian world.

. . . When the question arose concerning the most holy day of Easter it was decreed by common consent to be expedient, that this festival should be celebrated on the same day by all, in every place . . . And truly, in the first place, it seemed to every one a most unworthy thing that we should follow the custom of the Jews in the celebration of this most holy solemnity, who, polluted wretches, having stained their hands with a nefarious crime,

are justly blinded in their minds . . . It is fit, therefore, that rejecting the
practice of this people, we should perpetuate to all future ages the celebra-
tion of this rite, in a more legitimate order . . . Let us then have nothing
in common with the most hostile rabble of the Jews.

The Council, the first great Council of the Christian Church, now takes a sinister turn and validates a policy that is going to result in nothing less than persecution, leading to genocide, of the Jewish people for centuries to come. Our "One New Man" has been well and truly garotted. It's the start of a long slide away from the Jewish roots of the faith, with further Church Councils putting the boot in, again and again. The Council of Antioch in AD 345 threatened excommunication for any Christian celebrating Passover with the Jews. The Council of Laodicea in AD 365 extended this to all Jewish festivals as well as the Saturday Sabbath. The Jewish roots of the Christian faith had been well and truly sliced away and left rotting in the ground.

We have already seen, in our tour of the early Church, how Greek philosophical ideas wormed their way into Christian doctrine and Bible interpretation. But what we need to see now is less dry theory and dreary theology and more practical application. In other words, what was the outcome of these Greek influences? How does it affect us? Was it really that bad?

Our starting point is to return to the consequence of Plato's "Big Idea", probably the most influential pagan idea to infiltrate the Church.

Plato's Big Consequence: Soul = Good, Body = Bad

It may have been just one tiny idea, but it produced some major effects. Let's just think for a moment. The idea that spiritual things are good and physical things are bad first came to our attention when early Christian Bible teachers, like Origen and Augustine, started to look mainly for spiritual meanings all over the Bible, even when there weren't any. Any time they saw a passage and couldn't deal with the plain truth of the words, they would discard the literal meaning and seek for deeper meanings, through allegory.

For some, the Old Testament was just too down and dirty for their sensibilities. They reasoned that the God of the Old Testament, who created the evil *physical* world, was Plato's *Demiurge* and the nice *spiritual* God of the Christians was just the God of the New Testament. This was the view of an early heresy called *Marcionism*.

Then there was Jesus Himself. Another heresy called *Docetism* declared that God was a spiritual being and couldn't take a physical form. So Jesus couldn't possibly have had a real body, He just *seemed* to have one. He was therefore an illusion, as was the crucifixion! You can see how this *dualist* approach would have confused them. We know Jesus as fully God and fully man, but to these people, educated to believe that only "spiritual" is good, how can Jesus be expressed also in the "physical"? They just couldn't get their heads around it!

In fact heresies abounded in the first few centuries of the Christian era. Here are a few more. *Apollinarianism* stated that Jesus had a human body, a lower soul and a divine mind. *Eutychianism* suggested that Jesus' human nature was overcome by the divine nature. *Montanism* exercised a sort of extreme Pentecostalism. *Monarchianism* insisted that God was a single person. *Nestorianism* argued that Christ existed as two persons. *Sabellianism* declared that everything was how the believer perceived it to be, whatever that was meant to mean! They were either named after the person who thought them up or after the Greek word for the principal idea.

It is surely plain to see that this was the natural outcome of viewing Christianity as a philosophy rather than a pure faith. While Christian philosophers were debating Platonic principles applied to the Father, Son and Holy Spirit, their followers were killing each other in the name of the Father, Son and Holy Spirit (and Plato).

In the next chapter we are going to move away from such fringe interpretations and look to see how the mainstream Church took on these ideas from Greek philosophy and what the outcome was for Christians from those days to our days.

Things Ain't What
They Seem

With children, sometimes it's best to keep them in ignorance about certain things, because their minds are not ready for the leap from fantasy to reality and, of course, Santa Claus, the tooth fairy and various "bogey men" have their part to play in our parenting box of tricks. But what about us adults? How do we respond if we are suddenly told that there are a lot of things which are not what they seem to be? I am speaking here of the way we "do church".

How would you react to new ideas? Are you prepared to rethink and re-evaluate? I say this because this chapter may shock or surprise, as it deals with how Greek thinking has wormed its way into the very fabric of our Christian life. So consider yourself pre-warned, it may be an uncomfortable journey, in the same way that a tissue biopsy is uncomfortable, but vitally important in uncovering nasty things that need to be dealt with.

If you were to ask me to single out the most startling fact uncovered during the research for this book it would be the following.

Virtually every Christian reference book, when speaking of influences during the formative years of the Church, agrees and accepts that Greek philosophical ideas were key to the understanding of the fundamental doctrines.

No criticism or regret, just blithe acceptance, as if the pagan polluting of the faith in Jesus Christ is just one of those things, as if the Bible alone was not sufficient for our understanding of God and His dealings with mankind!

Nevertheless, the great majority of the Christian philosophers down to St. Augustine were Platonists. They appreciated the uplifting influence of Plato's psychology and metaphysics, and recognised in that influence a powerful ally of Christianity in the warfare against materialism and naturalism.
(*Catholic Encyclopaedia* – Life of Plato)

My goodness, when I think of the trouble the Jews got into for absorbing too much of the world into their lives during Old Testament times! Boy, did they suffer then – military failure, famine and exile, for marrying out and bowing to the odd stone idol. Their sacrifice was ultimately not in vain as they provided the environment and culture that ensured that the Messiah would be born into the world (though many Jews may argue this point).

The Jews endured a history of disappointment and suffering, but they kept their Scriptures pure and remained true to their God, enabling the Saviour to be born, live and die as fulfilment of prophecy. Then came the Church, the followers of that very same Jewish Saviour and, because it failed to remain pure and sullied itself with pagan philosophies, ensured that the Jews were going to continue to suffer for hundreds of years (more of that later). This is surely one of the great ironies of history.

But the Church had moved on from that pure, simple and effective vehicle for spreading the true Gospel of Jesus Christ at the time of the Book of Acts. Those simple core beliefs were to become submerged in a sea of philosophy and debate. It appears that Christians were more prepared to debate the true nature of the Holy Spirit than to see him in action, drawing people to a faith in Jesus Christ. To see how this happened we return again to Plato's "Big Consequence".

Plato's Big Consequence: Soul = Good, Body = Bad

We have seen how this affected their reading of the Bible and their theology of the Godhead, but what about how they saw themselves in God's eyes?

For a start, the immediate effect of declaring the body as bad and soul as good is an obvious one. If the body is bad then so are things associated with the body, particularly voluntary processes like sex. To the early Church, those who followed "spiritual" careers, in the Church, were expected to be celibate, a practice that continues to the modern-day Catholic Church and which has indirectly cost the Vatican millions of dollars in compensation claims (figure that one out for yourself). Monks were all required to be celibate and some of them were even resistant to the idea of taking a bath, in case they saw themselves naked! A Catholic view is still that celibacy is a "higher calling", in the sense of remaining pure until heaven beckons, when you will be united with Christ directly. Of course I am not proposing a 1960s-style sexual revolution for Christians. The early Church may have had muddled ideas regarding sex for the clergy, but one thing is absolutely clear – sex is an activity that can only be indulged in within the sacredness of the marriage covenant. Or, in other words, sex outside marriage for Christians is a complete no-no!

Then there were the flagellants and their like, who believed that only by scourging or whipping themselves could they achieve favour with God. They tended to appear during the plague seasons, such as during the Black Death in Europe, when they marched through the lands, whipping and beating themselves, in a misplaced idea of atoning for the sins of the world and appeasing an "angry" God.

So the ideas of Plato had convinced the Church that anything associated with our physical bodies was bad. It devalues our lives on Earth and fixes the idea in our minds that we should not place any worth in our earthly existence and yearn for heaven. You've heard the expression of *being so heavenly minded that you're no earthly good* and you can blame Plato's influence on this! It encourages us to see our faith just as a "ticket to heaven" rather than the service we are meant to give in this world, particularly in the context of the Great Commission. Of course, heaven is our great hope and reward, but that should not be at the expense of a fulfilled life, of service, sacrifice and testimony.

Here lies the real problem. Declaring a division between heaven and Earth, between sacred work and secular work, between the holy and the profane, between clergy and laity, between the supernatural and the natural, is a thoroughly Greek idea, coming from this *dualism* of Plato. It leads to a separation between "spiritual" occupations and the rest and have given us an unconscious respect for those of us with a *higher calling*. It fuels such attitudes as believing that missionaries, church workers, clergy and those "called out for Christian service" are the only real full-time Christians there are. The rest of us, working in offices, schools, building sites and the like, are "part-time" Christians, defined by what we do for God *away* from the workplace.

This idea is so prevalent today and is so wrong! If you are a born-again Christian then the Bible tells you that you are:

The Church

> *"So Peter was kept in prison, but the church was earnestly praying to God for him."*
> (Acts 12:5)

The Church is *not* a building, it is you and me, the people of God.

Priests

> *"To him who loves us and has freed us from our sins by his blood, and has made us to be a kingdom and priests to serve his God and Father – to him be glory and power for ever and ever! Amen."*
> (Revelation 1:6)

We are all priests, because we all have access to God through Jesus, by the power of the Holy Spirit. Yet many of us act as if this is not true, we still shove our pastors, teachers, preachers, worship leaders and even Christian celebrities onto pedestals and conference platforms and look to them to minister to us and show us Jesus. This is a thoroughly Greek idea and wrong! We don't need these people to "offer sacrifices" on our behalf, we are all priests and we can all approach Jesus directly.

Saints

> *"To all in Rome who are loved by God and called to be saints: Grace and peace to you from God our Father and from the Lord Jesus Christ."*
> (Romans 1:7)

We don't need to venerate dead bones or those who have cast off their mortal coil in glorious triumph. Dead saints can't hear your prayers, only God can. We are all saints, even though we may not always act very saintly. We are no less special than anyone else who has gone before us.

We are the Church, we are all priests and saints. We *all* have a higher calling. There is no sacred and secular, because we are all sacred, we all have a sacred calling.

> *"If anyone destroys God's temple, God will destroy him; for God's temple is sacred, and you are that temple."*
> (1 Corinthians 3:17)

Greek thinking tells us that the missionary, who travels overseas to work in a Christian village, showing God's love to those who haven't experienced it, is to be especially revered. Not to demean the sacrifice these people have made and the hardships they will undoubtedly endure, is this any different to those of you with a standard 9 to 5 job in an office, working in a thoroughly (and often aggressively) non-Christian environment, where any attempt at communicating your faith would be met with hostility, exclusion and even law suits? Who has the higher calling? Neither, because wherever we are in the world we are called to be witnesses.

All that God expects of us is to "be in the world but not of the world". We are to be salt and light in our witness to the world, without being sucked into its ways. Not easy and getting harder all the time! James reminds us of the consequences.

" . . . *don't you know that friendship with the world is hatred toward God? Anyone who chooses to be a friend of the world becomes an enemy of God."*
(James 4:4)

And speaking of work, we hear a lot of folk working to live rather than living to work. Given the choice, most of us would prefer to work less and play more. Well that's a Greek idea too, devaluing the act of working for a living and encouraging us to look forwards to weekends, when the real living takes place! *Let's party* is the mantra of today, borne from the Greek lifestyle philosophy of *hedonism*. The Ancient Greeks were people of leisure, manual work was left to the slaves. For Jews it was a lot different – for some of their history they *were* the slaves – but that's not the point I wish to make. The pattern of their attitude was set in the second chapter of the Bible.

"By the seventh day God had finished the work he had been doing; so on the seventh day he rested from all his work."
(Genesis 2:2)

God wasn't afraid to pull His sleeves up and get on with it. He expected man to do the same.

"The LORD God took the man and put him in the Garden of Eden to work it and take care of it."
(Genesis 2:15)

There is great satisfaction in working, a sense of earning your keep and adding to the common good. It is also God's plan for us. He didn't create us to spend our lives in selfish pursuits, leisure time and entertainment should be a reward for our toil, not an end in itself. Unfortunately many in the Church today act as if it is. *Did you enjoy the worship today? No, not really, perhaps we should go to a livelier church!*

Having attacked one or two sacred cows I may as well upset the whole herd now. There's nothing special about a church building. It's just a place where Christians hang out. It's no more or less sacred or holy than anywhere else. The altar is just a table for bread and wine. The act of Communion is holy but the elements of the process are just ordinary old bread and wine. These ideas are all from Greece, telling us that what we deem as "spiritual", even a building for meeting, is to be sought after. In fact God doesn't just float around waiting to be summoned by his flock into certain chosen acceptable places. God is every-where, even in brothels, crack dens and the White House, just as Jesus never hesitated in visiting places that the religious elite wouldn't dream of setting foot in.

"While Jesus was having dinner at Matthew's house, many tax collectors and 'sinners' came and ate with him and his disciples. When the Pharisees saw this, they asked his disciples, 'Why does your teacher eat with tax collectors and "sinners"?'"
(Matthew 9:10–11)

Then there is what we do when we're inside church. How do many of us get our instructions in Christian life and theology?

It's the sermon, of course! Yet the sermon didn't really catch on until the fourth century AD, around the same time that Greek ideas were beginning to take grip in the Church. Not a co-incidence, I'm afraid. The origins are with the *Sophists*, itinerant speakers who, dressed in their finery, gave impressive monologues, either in public squares or in exclusive dinner parties. This tradition was still alive at the time when the Christian Church was flourishing under official patronage and when many of these accomplished orators became Christians, many became paid preachers in the Church circuits of the day. This caught on, as these orators were skilled and polished in their art, masters of Greek rhetoric and soon only these trained individuals were allowed to preach to the masses. The mass impartation of Christian knowledge became a one-way street, delivered only by those with training in Greek rhetoric and oration. The sermons delivered were known as *homilies*, a word that still survives in the Church.

Now I am not saying that there is no place in Christian life for the sermon. Far from it! Jesus Himself preached enough of them, *the Sermon on the Mount* being a good example. And so did Peter and Paul in the Book of Acts. Noah himself was called a "preacher of righteousness" in 2 Peter 2:5, leading a whole line of biblical preachers who spoke out God's Word to the people. But there are sermons and there are "sermons". Done correctly, it has been God's favoured way of preaching the Word.

But it hasn't always been done correctly and there are plenty of "preachers" who have more to do with the Greek Sophists than the practitioners of the noble art of preaching. The modern-day Sophists stand there at the pulpit, perfectly groomed, teeth flashing with an earnest expression. Showmanship and cleverness are the priorities, rather than a humble and powerful exposition of God's Word. We must learn discernment at the very least. So how do we do this? When the preacher lifts his hands to God, look to see how many fingers are pointing back to him, figuratively speaking of course.

So let's not bash the sermon, but just be wary of the abuses and hold onto the thought that perhaps there are also other ways to convey the message of the Gospel. More about those later on.

Who usually preaches the sermon in today's Church? The pastor. This individual is mentioned just once in the New Testament,

> *"It was he who gave some to be apostles, some to be prophets, some to be evangelists, and some to be pastors and teachers."*
> (Ephesians 4:11)

The word *pastor* comes from the Greek word for "shepherd", referring to an individual who would care for his flock. Of course pastors perform this function, but they tend also to be the administrator, leader, teacher, preacher etc., etc. It is the Church's equivalent of the secular CEO, the top of the heap, the head of the hierarchy, the man with the desk slogan, "the buck stops here". Before the pastor was established, the early Church had no titles or offices or complex hierarchies. Everything was done in an informal manner by the elders and apostles. Then in a process started by Ignatius of Antioch, in the first century, a hierarchy slowly began to take shape within the Church, with the bishop taking on more and more responsibilities. He became the equivalent of today's pastor, as leader and spokesman, with his finger in every pie. The word *clergy*, referring to the people who did all the work in the Church, started to appear, as well as *laity*, referring to everyone else and the die was cast in separating "professional" Christians from the rest of us.

So the Church developed hierarchies, great human edifices that served to distance the common man from his God. Christians were no longer a "priesthood of all believers" (1 Peter 2:9) and access to God was now controlled by the middle-men of the clergy, who controlled every aspect of life and became a privileged caste of society, even exempt from paying taxes or serving in the army.

Sunday, when most of us go to Church, is just a day of the week, incidentally named after the Sun god (the emperor Constantine called it *the venerable day of the Sun*). Are we just Sunday Christians? If we are then we are just closet Greeks. We are saying that our times for personal holiness are just that hour or two on Sunday morning and the rest of the week belongs to us. Those Church visiting times are not particularly special to God, what He wants from us is 24/7 reality, lives dedicated to worshipping and serving Him even at 7.30pm on a Monday when our favourite soap is on the box.

This chapter has been nothing more than a small introduction to a very large subject. More could be said, but there is no need to do this, as I believe my point has been made. The Christian Church is far more Greek in its outlook than people could ever imagine and this is not a side issue, but very much a key battleground for the truth. This is not a battle, but a full-on war for the Christian heart and mind and you have only really been introduced to one side of the conflict. Now meet the cavalry . . .

PART TWO
Signs

"Jews demand miraculous signs . . . "
(1 Corinthians 1:22)

The Kosher Cavalry Arrives

You've met the Greeks and seen the harmful effects of their ideas on the Christian Church. Let's now venture into the lost Hebrew world of the Bible. Here is a declaration. It is God's big consequence:

God's Big Consequence: Soul = Good, Body = Good

This is a lost truth, corrupted by the ideas of Plato, who could not square up the physical world and the spiritual world. Here's the truth, from God's mouth to your ears, everything is good! The Jews knew it, in fact they still do.

The Hebraic and biblical view of our human existence is a holistic one, a seamless unity of mind, body and spirit. All are good and beneficial to our well-being. For example, there's nothing crude and un-godlike about our bodily functions.

> *"Blessed be the LORD God, King of the Universe, who has created humans with wisdom, with openings and hollow parts, revealed before Your holy throne, that if any part of the body was to malfunction, it would be impossible for us to exist and stand before You even for a short time. You cure all flesh and perform wonders!"*

Yes, this is the Jewish prayer for going to the toilet. All in life is a gift from God. Opening one's bowels regularly is a blessing (that's one for us oldies!), no more or less than eating or receiving an answered prayer. All should be thanked for and all are present in the Jewish liturgy. Plato would roll over in his earthy grave if he were ever exposed to this most earthy of prayers.

To religious Jews, everything in life is important to God, so it is important to involve Him in all parts of everyday life.

Prayer for waking up:

"I give thanks before You, Living and Eternal King, who has returned within me my soul with compassion; great is Your faithfulness!"

Here's another one:

"Blessed are You, HaShem, our God, King of the Universe, Who has this in His universe."

This prayer is quite warming. It's what you tell God when you see an exceptionally beautiful person, tree, or field. There's an even more warming variation on this:

"Blessed are You, HaShem, our God, King of the Universe, Who makes the creatures different."

This is what you tell God when you see exceptionally strange-looking people or animals. You see, to the Jewish eye, everything in this world is of interest to God, not just the "spiritual" stuff.

There are Jewish prayers that honour genuine scholarship, whether "sacred" or "secular". On seeing an outstanding Torah (Bible) teacher, there's this prayer:

"Blessed are You, HaShem, our God, King of the Universe, Who has apportioned of His knowledge to those who revere Him."

But there's also one on seeing an outstanding secular scholar. Note the subtle difference in wording:

"Blessed are You, HaShem, our God, King of the Universe, Who has given of His knowledge to flesh and blood."

Of course any prayer that is offered out of habit and ritual rather than a genuine desire to communicate with God is probably as useless as a burnt offering. It is always going to be a matter of the heart and will, but the general principle is that, in acknowledgement of the fact that God has a passionate interest in all facets of our existence, we have a directory of prayers to draw upon.

For most Christians the only time a prayer is offered for an everyday act is our Grace before a meal. Is it because we believe that God only wants to hear from us in church, quiet times or prayer meetings? God doesn't keep to an appointment book, His door is always open, even when we've had success in the lavatory!

While we're talking about bodily functions, now is a good time to think about one of the most confusing things of all – what exactly is the relationship between the mind, body, soul and spirit? The reason it is confusing is that the Church has always tried to explain it by marrying together biblical concepts with Greek understanding. The result is a plethora of views and definitions. The alternative is to look at it from a totally biblical viewpoint, the Jewish way. So what's the problem?

Greek duality insists that we start with the position that the body is bad and the mind, soul and spirit are good. On death, both parts separate and the "mortal" body is discarded and the "immortal" mind/soul/spirit, that is the *real you*, moves on. The Greek understanding is that only by the shedding of the "evil" body can we be with God, as immortal spiritual beings in heaven. This view may seem acceptable to you, it may even be what you have been taught, but it is *not* biblical.

Biblically, human beings are whole beings, body and soul together. We need our bodies, which is why, when we die, we eventually have a *bodily* resurrection, body and soul returning together and living on Earth! It's a strange concept, alien to how we've been taught, but it's as biblical as the virgin birth and the feeding of the 5,000, also strange concepts to our carnal logical minds. If you still don't believe me, read the very end of the Bible, Revelation chapters 21 and 22. Here's a spoiler.

"I saw the Holy City, the new Jerusalem, coming down out of heaven from God, prepared as a bride beautifully dressed for her husband. And I heard a loud voice from the throne saying, 'Now the dwelling of God is with men, and he will live with them. They will be his people, and God himself will be with them and be their God.'"
(Revelation 21:2–3)

This is the end of the End. God is living *on Earth* with His people. Just picture that!

So, Hebraically (and biblically) speaking, what is the difference between body, soul and spirit? Our problem is that Greek thinking has compartmentalised all of these aspects of a human being, but drawn very fuzzy lines between them. How many of us can really tell the difference between the soul and the spirit? And what about the mind, the heart and the emotions, where do they fit in?

On the face of it, this is no easy task. In the Bible, the Hebrew word, *nephesh*, is translated as "soul" around 470 times, but is also translated as "life", "mind", "person", "heart" as well as over twenty other possibilities. The Hebrew word, *ruach*, is translated as "spirit" around 240 times, but is also translated as "breath", "wind" and about ten other possibilities. As we will learn in a later chapter, the Hebrew language is very evocative and helps us to understand difficult concepts by getting a grasp of all possible meanings of a word.

So, we can now look at the word for "soul" and, by looking at the other possible translations – "life", "mind", "person" and "heart" – we can get the impression, Hebraically, that the soul is what makes you, "you". It refers to the whole person, body included. The soul does not exist apart from the body, so the concept of ghosts as "lost souls" floating around without bodies and scaring you witless, is a complete nonsense!

When we consider our "spirit", we are looking at something that is "breathed" into man. So man is a soul, but is *not* a spirit, though he *has* a spirit.

> *"Moreover, we have all had human fathers who disciplined us and we respected them for it. How much more should we submit to the Father of our spirits and live!"*
> (Hebrews 12:9)

The spirit is from God and we all have it, though in most of us it is dead. Let me explain. God breathed His Spirit into the first man, Adam. When Adam sinned, his spirit died and ever since then men and women are spiritually dead. That is, until they allow the Holy Spirit to connect up and quicken their spirits through a new birth in Jesus Christ.

> *"But if Christ is in you, your body is dead because of sin, yet your spirit is alive because of righteousness. And if the Spirit of him who raised Jesus from the dead is living in you, he who raised Christ from the dead will also give life to your mortal bodies through his Spirit, who lives in you."*
> (Romans 8:10–11)

As far as the emotions are concerned, there are numerous scriptures that place these either with the soul or the spirit. There are no clear cut lines of demarcation here.

This is a HUGE subject, with volumes of Scripture to illustrate many of the points made. There is simply no room here to say much more, otherwise the thrust of this book will be lost, but just keep in mind the fact that, whereas Greek thinking ties you up in a constant state of over-analysis, the Hebrew mindset is more forgiving but asks you to hold on to the basic truth that the body and soul together make up a human being and the spirit is what connects us to God.

In fact it is very difficult for us twenty-first century folk to burst out of the thought patterns that permeate our society, our education system, our everyday life. We think in Greek ways, that is the legacy of history, it is not easy to think in any other ways. But let me see if I can express the leap we would have to make, in order to start thinking *Hebraically*.

The Greek mind says that man is at the centre of life, the Hebrew mind says that God is at the centre of life. The Greek mind says that the things of God must be deduced from our logical minds, the Hebrew mind says that the things of God can only be understood by faith and revelation. The Greek mind says that we should strive for knowledge *about* God, the Hebrew mind says that we should *know* God.

These are just words and concepts, we need to let them really sink in and soak us in their truths. It may take time, but it will be worth it. Just think of that last one again. I will repeat it.

The Greek mind says that we should strive for knowledge about God, the Hebrew mind says that we should know God.

Think about it. The Greek part of us inclines us towards building us a whole library of books, podcasts and sermons that help us to build up a *systematic theology* of God, an understanding of His attributes. The Hebrew part of us inclines us to drop to our knees and ask Him to teach us His ways. The Greek part of us inclines us to read Bible commentaries, benefiting from the wisdom of scholars. The Hebrew part of us inclines us to read the Bible alone and pray for revelation and illumination.

So we have now entered the world of Hebrew thought. It's worth pausing at this moment to think through the implications of the Hebraic (biblical) worldview up against the prevailing Greek mindset. Although I may have laboured the point, it is key that we fully understand the main implication of Platonic thought, the idea of separation between the evil physical world and the good spiritual world. It runs counter to the biblical thought that it replaced, the *holistic* view of things, where the spiritual and physical should be seen working together as a whole.

What now follows in the next few chapters is a series of vignettes, highlighting different aspects of the Hebraic world-view. We will look at Jewish festivals, the Hebrew language and views of God, family life and religious practices. But first we think more about the Book where our Christian doctrines should be coming from. We start by looking at the Bible itself.

Thus Sayeth the Lord . . . Allegedly!

So much to say, so little time. How to read the Bible has got to be the key to everything, so isn't it amazing how often we get it wrong! For the Christian it is the source of all our knowledge and the rulebook for all our practices. My task is to condense a library topic into a single chapter, so don't expect a thorough treatment, but rather the exploration of a single strand, personi-fied by this question: *What can Jewish scholarship tell us about our approach to God's Word?* But first, a rant!

If there's one single issue that confuses Christian folk most when it comes to reading and understanding the Bible, it's what to do with the Old Testament. Is it still relevant to Christians today? Is it equal in inspiration to the New Testament? Is it liter-ally true? Is it just for Jews? Is it full of hidden and secret truths to be teased out through arcane knowledge of codes, Hebrew structures or numerological manipulations? We need to know, once and for all, because there are preachers and teachers out there who are using the Old Testament in ways that surely would have Jesus turning in His grave, if He had one!

Let us take a case study to illustrate this. A certain TV preach-er's technique is to take a Jewish religious festival and, through a random mangling of scriptures "connected" to this festival, "proves" that anyone who sends in their cash will be blessed in all sorts of ways and indeed will attain a guaranteed financial return from the "Bank of God". He does this secure in the knowledge that most viewers have little relevant knowledge to query his findings and are simply seduced by his showmanship. Here is what he did.

His target was the Feast of Tabernacles, *Sukkot*. Not dwelling on the mispronunciations and misapplications of many Jewish terms he used, the crux of his argument was linking Joel chapter 2 with the festival. The first point to make is that there are scriptures connected to Sukkot. There are the primary verses that explicitly describe the festival, in Leviticus 23:33–43, Numbers 29:12–39 and Deuteronomy 16:13–17. Then there are other associated readings in Ecclesiastes, Psalms and Zechariah. But nowhere in Hebrew Scripture or Jewish Tradition do the verses in Joel chapter 2 have any relevance to Sukkot.

So in the first place he was taking a totally unrelated scripture. The passage he dwelt on was Joel 2:18–27. In its context the passage has Joel promising the people of Israel that God would restore things to them if they repent. It was not too late for them. Now this has nothing to do with the theme or the setting of Sukkot. So how did he connect the two scriptures? He did so by taking one short phrase and totally misusing it – we can only assume he did this out of ignorance rather than cunning intent.

> *"Be glad then, ye children of Zion, and rejoice in the* Lord *your God: for he hath given you the former rain moderately, and he will cause to come down for you the rain, the former rain, and the latter rain* **in the first month.***"*
>
> (Joel 2:23 KJV, emphasis added)

He took the phrase "in the first month" and assumed that this was referring to the month of Tishrei, the autumn month of the Jewish *civil* New Year, the month of Sukkot, the Feast of Tabernacles.

There's a big problem with this. Never in the Bible is the first month *anything other* than Nisan, in spring, the time of Passover.

So we could actually stop here because we have taken away the whole foundation of his argument – his tenuous and faulty link between Joel chapter 2 and the Feast of Tabernacles. But it actually gets worse. Here is verse 19:

> *"Yea, the Lord will answer and say unto his people, Behold, I will send you corn, and wine, and oil, and ye shall be satisfied therewith: and I will no more make you a reproach among the heathen."*
>
> (KJV – the version he was using)

Here is his take on the first part of this verse: *Yea, the Lord will answer and say unto his people, Behold, I will send you money, and blessing, and anointing (so no weapon may prosper against you).*

So, according to him, these are the rewards you will receive. And how will you receive them? Another scripture twist, in verse 23:

> *"Be glad then, ye children of Zion, and rejoice in the Lord your God . . . "*
>
> (KJV)

His take on *rejoicing* is for you to send money to the ministry that he was working for. Rejoicing implies action and God clearly intended this to be your reaching for your wallet. Only by doing so will you unlock these financial blessings, which will also include a *double portion* (how he arrived at that is totally indecipherable) for you.

Please, please God protect us from these "teachers". Amen. Enough is enough, it is time we took the Bible seriously. God's Holy word of encouragement, enrichment and truth for mankind cannot and must not be used as a recipe book for manipulation.

So what have we learned from this? How can we guard against these misuses? Well, one sign to take heed of is when someone tells you that God *has spoken prophetically* to him, using Scripture. *God spoke to me prophetically.*

This is a huge topic and disappointingly off-subject to the narrative I am building. I will simply pose one unanswered question. *If God allows certain people to re-interpret His precious words, how can we ever discern who is speaking the truth?* Either there are tried and tested ways of reading and acting on the Bible or God has removed all barriers and declared open season and a free-for-all. Which option sounds like the God that you and I worship? Answers on a postcard please!

God provided us with a Bible, at an incredible cost for its many cast members, many of whom suffered or died so that we can learn from their lives, their mistakes and their triumphs. Many also suffered and died through history, just for preserving this Book, even for translating it into English. It's a precious book, God knows that, all serious Christians know that. So to see the many ways it has been mangled, twisted and re-interpreted by some for their own purposes is just unacceptable. There are enough people who claim to have new revelations and new interpretations and we must learn to recognise when this is happening and reject it. The Bible has only one author, God, and the task we have is to know exactly what is in His heart as we read His words.

So how do we read and interpret the Bible? How can we tell what is in the heart of God as we read His words? We begin with two Greek words, *exegesis* and *eisegesis*. Exegesis is the act of reading the words of the Bible and receiving the truth that God put there. Eisegesis is the act of reading the words of the Bible and only receiving what agrees with your own ideas. The first technique is, I hope you agree, the way we should approach the Bible. The other one is the chosen route of our TV preacher and may God forgive him!

Surely we all want to read the words of the Bible and receive the truth that God put there. So where do we start? Let's start in the Bible itself.

*"For Ezra had devoted himself to the study and observance of the Law
of the LORD, and to teaching its decrees and laws in Israel."*
(Ezra 7:10)

Ezra took seriously the study of the written Word of God. The
Hebrew word used, translated as "study and observance" is
darash. Ezra was the spiritual leader who led the Jews from exile
in Babylon to Jerusalem and got them all reading their Scriptures!
From this period in history we can trace the beginnings of
synagogues, where Scriptures are read out and expounded on.

So our starting point must be with these Jews who were first
blessed with the Word of God. We would do well, at this point,
to remember what Paul said of the Jewish people.

*"Theirs is the adoption as sons; theirs the divine glory, the covenants, the
receiving of the law, the temple worship and the promises. Theirs are
the patriarchs, and from them is traced the human ancestry of Christ,
who is God over all, forever praised! Amen."*
(Romans 9:4–5)

The Bible that Jesus knew was written by Hebrews, for Hebrews
and about Hebrews, in the Hebrew and Aramaic languages,
using Hebrew idioms, poetic styles and writing styles. So a good
place to start when trying to understand the Bible is to turn to
the Jewish Jesus Himself.

So far we have not strayed too far from the orthodox teaching
on how to understand the Bible. It is called the *Grammatical
Historic method* and all it means is that we put ourselves in the
role of someone who would have heard the words in the original
setting and how they would have understood the words in
context. So, all we need to do is pretend we are a first-century
Jew with an understanding of first-century Jewish stuff. Not
easy is it? No, but we can at least make an effort!

There are rules used by Jewish scholars in reading and understanding Scripture. These have been developed over a period of

time by groups of scholars who, at the same time, were creating huge commentaries on the Bible, compiled into such volumes as the Talmud. As interesting as this is, it doesn't help us, as we are looking for tools that the modern Western mind can understand and use, not dreary old reference books to leaf through. We have enough of those in the Christian world!

Unfortunately we start off at a disadvantage. Jesus and His contemporaries, in common with Jews before Him and after Him, would have had an encyclopaedic knowledge of the Hebrew Scriptures, the Old Testament. Jewish boys would study the Torah (the first five books of the Bible) at the age of five, the oral "Traditions" at the age of ten and be trained in *halachot*, rabbinic legal decisions, at the ripe old age of fifteen! Scripture would be memorised as they didn't have laptops in those days, or even ready access to writing materials. They knew God's Word like some of us know the Simpsons, past storylines of our favourite soaps, or the traits and foibles of the latest movie star. Many of us struggle to come up with just the basic facts of standard Bible stories, particularly if we weren't carted off to Sunday school when children. We just don't, by and large, have an instinctive grasp of the Hebrew Scriptures and, consequently, we are handicapped when it comes to using traditional Jewish tools for understanding God's Word.

But there is hope for us. They may have had the biblical training from a young age, but we have computers and these electronic companions can simulate a whole lifetime of study and experience. It's both sad and handy, but we must look on the bright side and use whatever tools we have at our disposal!

Jesus did a lot of stuff. Virtually everything He did was to fulfil the words of prophets of an earlier age. He healed, He taught, He comforted, He corrected, He put people right with God. In doing so He was able to point to His actions as fulfilments to the writings of Isaiah, Jeremiah, the Psalms and many other places. He was able to do so because there was a general agreement among the Jews of His day as to what these scriptures were saying. They knew how to make sense of their Scriptures. The question of interpretation was not an issue as they all shared the same tools for reading these sacred words. Not so, today. Over the last two thousand years of Christianity we have developed so many ways of reading and interpreting the Bible, it seems that we can make scriptures say whatever we want them to say, without any regard to what they are actually saying. As a result, unscrupulous men have got rich, dastardly acts have been committed and communities have been led astray. All because "the Bible says . . . "

It seems to me that when confusion and uncertainty reign, then going back to origins is no bad thing. As Christians, who do we take as the ultimate authority? Jesus, of course. Then surely, in terms of the Scriptures available to Him in His day (the Old Testament), we must read them through the eyes of Jesus, a first-century Jew. To do this we don't necessarily need a knowledge of Hebrew and Aramaic, the written languages of Scripture in those days. What we do need is to get inside their heads and follow the thought processes that drove their understanding.

It would help if, say among the Dead Sea Scrolls, someone found a set of parchments under the heading of "Reading Scripture the Jesus way" or "Bible interpretation for the non-Hebrew mind". We are not given this luxury but we can piece together a good picture from fragments of information from various sources, either from that time itself or from later writings. So where do we start?

There's a buzzword in the world of Jewish Bible interpretation. It's a Hebrew word, *pardes*, meaning "orchard". It's an acronym, but a dangerous one, as it derives from medieval Jewish mysticism, but we can still use it now that we have the knowledge of its origins. It's an acronym of four Jewish methods of Bible interpretation – *p'shat*, *remez*, *d'rash* and *sod*. It's the final component, *sod*, that provides the mystical element, delving into the area of secret meanings and numerical codes. Some of this is probably quite harmless and possibly even faith-building, but no-one is going to accuse me of leading folk astray, so out come the secateurs and, like any good gardener, my orchard has been well and truly pruned! Out goes the sod.

This leaves us with three methods of biblical interpretation and we shall look at each in turn.

First we have *p'shat*, a word that means "simple rendering" and encourages us to first take the plain simple meaning of the Scripture you are reading. This is easy, no computers needed here. In fact this method is basically the same as the traditional Christian method mentioned earlier, the *Grammatical Historic method*. In this you take the literal meaning of the text – the plain sense of what you are reading – with attention given to the grammar (the form of the words), the context (looking at the other verses before and after this one) and the historical meaning (who is talking, who is he talking to, where they are talking and when they were talking).

This is reading the Bible in the same way as we read anything, from a trashy novel to a motorcycle maintenance manual. We take the plain sense of what we are reading. When Lady Alice decides to take her butler Geoffrey on a cruise of the South Seas, we assume they are booking tickets on a liner rather than sharing some metaphysical vision. When you are warned against the engine oil of your motorbike falling below the minimum level, we are talking about a straightforward physical measure-ment, rather than an issue of the quality of the oil or making an allegorical statement about your moral standing. When God makes promises to Abraham about his descendants and where they will live, we can assume that is exactly what He is talking about, in its literal sense. That's how Jesus would have seen it.

The second method is *remez*, meaning "to hint". This goes a bit deeper and takes us into the areas of typology (where some-thing in the Old Testament connects with something later on in the New Testament), symbolism (where something in the Old Testament represents something else) and allegory (which you have already met). Beware murky waters, because sharks and other predators lurk within, seeking to devour you. Because once we veer away from the safety of *p'shat* and its literal meaning we can fall prey to those (like our TV preacher) who claim special understandings. This is a minefield, not only because of the charlatans of the Christian world but because of certain interpretations of Scripture that have been passed down from generation to generation, using the mind-set and tools developed by our Greek philosophers and their Christian devotees.

But let's look at Jesus. He made good use of *remez*. Along with all observant Jews of His day, He would have been thoroughly acquainted with Holy Scripture, which at that time was what we call the Old Testament. Much of it was committed to memory from an early age, particularly as most Jews did not have access to parchments of the written words. There was great zeal for the Word of God. Of course they didn't have the distractions that face us today, competition from the television, radio, internet, books and other printed material. We fill our brains up with so much nonsense and trivia these days, it's a wonder that there's room left for God's Word to settle, marinate and inspire.

There are some people today, known by some as aficionados, by others as nerds, who have such an encyclopaedic knowledge of some piece of entertainment that reminding them of just a snippet of dialogue would trigger a deluge of recollection. For example, mention *tribbles* to a Trekkie or the *Ogron* to a Dr Who fanatic and they will provide you with programme details, first viewing date, cast members and selective dialogue for the relevant episode. Believe it or not Jesus and His contemporaries were of the same ilk. For example, when Jesus was castigating the religious leaders in the Temple and called the place "a den of robbers", His listeners' minds immediately latched onto a piece of Scripture in the Book of Jeremiah, which spoke of "a den of robbers", and the full significance of the words would have been drummed home.

Jesus made use here of a technique called *allusion*. He alluded to, or made reference to, other known scriptures in order to make a point. Because there was such a familiarity with Scripture, He only had to quote a few words from a verse to trigger whole passages of Scripture into His listeners' minds, from which the teaching point will be made. This is *remez* in action.

Here's another example. Consider this passage in Matthew, Jesus' escape to Egypt.

> *"When they had gone, an angel of the Lord appeared to Joseph in a dream. 'Get up,' he said, 'take the child and his mother and escape to Egypt. Stay there until I tell you, for Herod is going to search for the child to kill him.' So he got up, took the child and his mother during the night and left for Egypt, where he stayed until the death of Herod. And so was fulfilled what the Lord had said through the prophet:* **'Out of Egypt I called my son.'"**
> (Matthew 2:13–15, emphasis added)

Perhaps you have been confused by the last few words, *"Out of Egypt I called my son."* It seems to be referring to Jesus, already described in the Nativity narrative, in Matthew chapter 1, as God's Son.

The passage in Matthew chapter 2 states that this is a fulfilment of what the Lord said through a prophet. The prophet in mind is Hosea, who quoted God in the words:

> *"When Israel was a child, I loved him, and out of Egypt I called my son."*
> (Hosea 11:1)

Matthew stated that Jesus' return from Egypt fulfilled Hosea's prophecy, yet it clearly doesn't read that way – Hosea is speaking about Israel, not Jesus! So the *p'shat*, the plain reading of the Hosea verse does not square up with Matthew's words. So, instead we look at *remez* and ask whether a truth is being hinted at.

Jesus and other first-century Jews would have known that there are places in Scripture where Israel is seen as God's son:

> *"Then say to Pharaoh, 'This is what the* Lord *says: Israel is my firstborn son.'"*
> (Exodus 4:22)

> *"They will come with weeping; they will pray as I bring them back. I will lead them beside streams of water on a level path where they will not stumble, because I am Israel's father, and Ephraim is my firstborn son."*
> (Jeremiah 31:9)

So, when Matthew described Jesus' return from Egypt as *"Out of Egypt I called my son"*, his readers would see the connection with Hosea 11:1, the link being the idea of "God's son". It is a *remez*, a hint. By stating Jesus' return as a fulfilment of Hosea's prophecy, Matthew is reinforcing Jesus' role as God's real flesh-and-blood first-born Son.

Another form of *remez* would be going a little deeper and using the technique we have already heard about, *allegory*. We have seen these techniques when we looked at Origen and Augustine and how they derived their allegorical methods from the teachings of Plato. So is all allegory bad? There's a real danger of *throwing out the baby with the bath water*, as there is good allegory and bad allegory. In a nutshell, good allegory has been put there by God to give us a deeper truth and a bad allegory is the product of a human mind that either rejects the literal reading of the text and/or feels that they have a "special revelation" to interpret the text in a certain way.

Here is a good allegory. Jesus being referred to as the Lamb of God, or referring to Himself as the good shepherd. These can be backed up by Old Testament scriptures, from Isaiah and Ezekiel and connections can be made.

"He was oppressed and afflicted,
  yet he did not open his mouth;
he was led like a lamb to the slaughter,
  and as a sheep before her shearers is silent,
  so he did not open his mouth."
(Isaiah 53:7)

"My servant David will be king over them, and they will all have one
shepherd. They will follow my laws and be careful to keep my decrees."
(Ezekiel 37:24)

Then there is *bad* allegory . . . and we stumble into a minefield.
Of course, this is just my opinion and I will now state categori-
cally that I'm a *p'shat man*. I believe that, in common with Jesus
and the first-century Jewish Christians, the Bible is to be understood, in the first instance, in its literal sense, as *p'shat*. For those
who disagree, the only refuge is allegory. Either you believe in
the clear narrative of certain Bible passages, or you don't believe
them and spiritualise them as allegory. But there are consequences. I will now briefly rush through just three scenarios.

Creation
Either you believe in the literal six days of Creation or you see
it mostly as poetry. The consequence of a literal reading is
usually ridicule by the scientific community, the media and other
Christians. The consequences of an allegorical reading are an
unwillingness to believe that God could create the Universe with
such ease and intricacy and an acceptance of secular scientific
explanations as promoted by our educational system.

The Fall
Either you believe in a literal Adam and Eve and serpent
scenario or you believe that it's just a spiritualised story. The consequence of a literal reading is usually ridicule by the scientific
community, the media and other Christians. The consequence

of an allegorical reading is a confused theology that can't see Jesus as the "Last Adam", as the first never physically existed.

"So it is written: 'The first man Adam became a living being'; the last Adam, a life-giving spirit. The spiritual did not come first, but the natural, and after that the spiritual. The first man was of the dust of the earth, the second man from heaven."

(1 Corinthians 15:45–47)

Israel

Either you believe that Jews are still literally God's people (along with the Church) and the literal promises regarding the Land of Israel still stand or you don't and allegorise the Scriptures to imply God's "spiritual" people have replaced God's "natural" people (shades of *dualism* here, please note). The consequence of the latter position, known as Replacement Theology, has fuelled 1500 years of Christian anti-Semitism, leading to genocide, though it must be stated that not all who accept this theological position are Jew-haters.

This has just been a simplification of three areas that are hot topics in today's Church. All that I ask is that you re-examine your position on these topics and ask yourself if these are inherited beliefs or whether you have sincerely and prayerfully worked through the issues.

But let's move on, because there is one more technique used by Jewish scholars for Bible interpretation. This is *d'rash* or *midrash*. It means "to seek or search" and it implies going a little deeper in your Bible study. Early rabbis devised rules to use during this process, from the seven rules of Rabbi Hillel, to the thirteen rules of Rabbi Ishmael, then to the thirty two rules of Rabbi Eliezer. It's not a technique that would come naturally to you or me, it is unlikely that those of us brought up in Greek understandings of Scripture are going to get to the heart of midrashic techniques. It is one for the scholars and the specialists. Jesus, Himself, used *midrash*.

> *"You have heard that it was said, 'Do not commit adultery.' But I tell you that anyone who looks at a woman lustfully has already committed adultery with her in his heart."*
> (Matthew 5:27–28)

This saying uses a midrashic technique known as *kal vachomer*, meaning "light and heavy". What this really means is that *if a minor thing is true, then so would a major one, but more so*. Or, if something light is true (e.g. owing someone £100 is a problem), then something heavy is also true (e.g. owing £200 is a bigger problem). So, if lusting ("light") after someone is a sin, then how much more a sin would be the actual act of adultery ("heavy").

Jesus uses *kal vachomer* a lot and nowhere does it need to be understood more than in the following verses.

> *"If your right eye causes you to sin, gouge it out and throw it away. It is better for you to lose one part of your body than for your whole body to be thrown into hell. And if your right hand causes you to sin, cut it off and throw it away. It is better for you to lose one part of your body than for your whole body to go into hell."*
> (Matthew 5:29–30)

The essence is that if a sin can be nipped in the bud while it is still in its "light" stage (just your right hand) then you can be prevented from the implications of the "heavy" stage (going to hell). It is important to see these verses as a figurative example, rather than being taken literally, otherwise there would be a lot of Captain Hooks in heaven!

This is a big subject and I have barely skimmed the surface, but hopefully you now have a feel for Jewish techniques of Bible interpretation. Surely there's more to be gained by reading Scripture in the same mindset used by Jesus Himself, than that developed years later, derived from the ideas of Greek philosophy.

So now you have been introduced to how we can benefit in our walk with the Lord by reading the Bible the Jewish way. It can take us to exciting places. It encourages us to look at Scripture as Jesus did, unburdened by developments in the scientific secular world. By encouraging us to take Scripture in the first instance at face value we are invited to embrace truths that have been lost by many Christians these days, eager as they are to construct a faith in line with secular developments, in order to stay "relevant". Jesus was a Creationist. Jesus believed that His natural people, the Jews, had a prophetically significant future. How big is our faith? Dare we put the Bible first and ask God to guide our way through the jungles of ridicule? The ball is in your court.

Every Day with Yeshua, Every Year with God

For many, the passage of time only impinges on daily life at anniversaries, birthdays and New Year celebrations. These events have just one thing in common – they are strung together through the passage of a single year, twelve months, 365 days. The Church calendar seeks to graft meaning into this, basing its festivals and holy days explicitly on the life and times of Jesus Christ, as defined by tradition. The Jewish calendar is also locked into Jesus, but it doesn't realise it. It is also thoroughly biblical. A journey through the Jewish year is a series of Bible studies, spanning the Old and the New, with added fun, activity and plenty of food and drink. But first, we pause.

You may think you are ready for this journey through time, but perhaps you are not. This is because we have to make some mental preparations first, as the passage of time that we call a year depends on what heavenly body we use as reference. The Christian calendar that regulates our lives is governed by the Sun. We take a note of how long the Earth takes to travel once around the Sun and we call that a *year*. We also take note of how long it takes the Earth to revolve once around its axis and we call that a *day*. Now this would be a neat arrangement if an exact number of days exactly fitted into a year. In fact a year is 365 days, 5 hours, 49 minutes and 12 seconds. Can't we just round this down and sweep the odd bits and pieces under the carpet? Unfortunately not, because that would give us slippage, we'd always be starting a fresh year nearly six hours early. The problem will be that certain landmark days would keep shifting through the seasons and the big problem was the key Christian festival of Easter.

The dating of Easter is complex enough to demand a whole chapter but I'm going to simplify it by stating that it is determined by the position of both the Sun and the Moon and is a different day every year. The whole point is to anchor Easter in the correct season of spring, so that the Church calendar remains relevant. Even with the complex calculations that the Church uses to determine the date of Easter, it still doesn't work out on the same day every year. Surely Easter happened on a particular date in history, why can't we just celebrate it on the nearest Sunday to that date? Isn't God a God of order? So, if Easter was so important and it was linked closely with the position of the Moon, why not go the whole hog and base the whole calendar on the Moon? This brings us nicely to the Jewish calendar. Let us now begin our journey.

Our journey starts on a speed bump, a hiccup to slow us down, as it's not just the Sun that messes up our calculations, but the Moon too. The Jewish year is based on the movement of the Moon, called the Lunar Month, the time between the appearance of the first sliver of Moon in the night sky until its eventual disappearance. The year is made up of either 12 or 13 of these months, which will have either 29 or 30 days. I told you it was messy! Whereas the Christian calendar uses the addition of days on leap years to keep things stable, the Jewish has leap months, an extra month shoved into the year every now and again. OK, so it's a load of maths again, but there's a crucial difference between the Christian and Jewish calendar. If Easter were Jewish then at least it would fall on the same day every year. But it isn't Jewish and that leads us nicely to the start of the Jewish year.

The Bible measures time in a totally different way from us.

You'll be familiar with this formula in Scripture, repeated seven times as part of the Creation story in the first chapter of the Bible.

> *"And there was evening, and there was morning – the first [second, third etc.] day."*

We're only in the first part of the first part of the first part of the Bible, yet we can already see where the Church has veered away from the Bible. If it wasn't bad enough that we name our days after pagan deities (of Roman and Nordic origin), we don't even begin each day in the biblical manner. The Bible begins each day at sunset, not midnight and so does the Jewish calendar.

So where does the Jewish Year start? This *may* surprise some of you, but it doesn't actually start at the Jewish New Year! The festival known as *Rosh Hashanah*, the Jewish New Year, is *not* the start of the year according to the Bible, in fact it falls in the seventh month of the year! But more of that later, as we're going to concentrate on the *biblical* calendar, which is the same as the Jewish Calendar in every way except for the issue of when it starts.

The first month of the biblical calendar is *Nisan*. A good Hebrew name, soaked in arcane meaning and biblical significance? No, actually, it is a Babylonian name, as are all the Jewish months. Uncharacteristically, for a book that attaches such meanings to names, the Bible generally doesn't name any months at all, simply referring to them as the *first* month, *second* month etc. So why Babylonian names, already? The Rabbis tell us that they are to remind the Jews of the exile in Babylon. This is borne out by the fact that we only start to see names being used in the Bible in reference to events that happened after the return from Babylon.

> *"In the twelfth year of King Xerxes, in the first month, the month of Nisan, they cast the pur (that is, the lot) in the presence of Haman to*

select a day and month. And the lot fell on the twelfth month, the month of Adar."
(Esther 3:7)

There was an event in Jewish history considered far more important than the return from Babylon, an event of such importance that it actually kick-starts the biblical year. That event was the Exodus from Egypt, an event so pivotal, that God wanted to make sure that it was never forgotten and scattered the Bible with references to it. In fact, in many cases, this was how God defined Himself, to ensure that His people knew it was He that was speaking to them and working on their behalf. The form taken was of the type, *I am the Lord your God, who brought your people out of Egypt . . .*

Nisan always falls in early springtime, thanks to the "leap month" system mentioned earlier and that is where our journey starts. Our journey will take us through three parallel and intertwining themes, biblical events (in both Old and New Testaments), future promises and the seasons of nature and through it we will find our faith enriched as we marvel at God's unfolding plan for mankind.

God Himself gets the ball rolling.

"The LORD said to Moses and Aaron in Egypt, 'This month is to be for you the first month, the first month of your year.'"
(Exodus 12:1–2)

The scene is set. Four hundred and thirty years of slavery and hard labour in Egypt was about to come to an end. God has acted and salvation is literally days away. Nine plagues have failed to convince Pharaoh to let Moses lead his people out of Egypt and we are standing at the edge of history. Something significant is about to happen and God issues His instructions. On the day of Nisan 10th every Jewish family is to buy a lamb, a male lamb without defect . . .

"Tell the whole community of Israel that on the tenth day of this month each man is to take a lamb for his family, one for each household."
(Exodus 12:3)

Another scene flickers into view, in the Roman province of Judea, around fifteen centuries later. It is also Nisan 10th. On the eastern approach of Jerusalem a crowd gathers. They are celebrating the arrival of an honoured visitor. It is Jesus, Yeshua, riding on a donkey. It is His triumphal entry. This day is Palm Sunday in the Christian calendar (only rarely celebrated on the authentic date) and the *Lamb of God* has revealed Himself to His people.

"When Jesus entered Jerusalem, the whole city was stirred and asked, 'Who is this?'
The crowds answered, 'This is Jesus, the prophet from Nazareth in Galilee.'"
(Matthew 21:10–11)

God instructs His people through Moses that this lamb is to be kept out of harm's way, looked after by the family, for four days. Jesus also spent these four days teaching His family of disciples and wandering around Jerusalem speaking to whoever was willing to listen. These were days of safety, the calm before the storm.

The four days are up. It is now the evening and Nisan 14th now becomes Nisan 15th (remember, biblical days start in the evening) and God instructs that the lambs are to be slaughtered and to be roasted, eaten with bitter herbs and unleavened bread. He gives further instructions.

"Do not leave any of it till morning; if some is left till morning, you must burn it. This is how you are to eat it: with your cloak tucked into your belt, your sandals on your feet and your staff in your hand. Eat it in haste; it is the LORD's Passover."
(Exodus 12:10–11)

It is this Passover meal that is to save them from what is about to happen. The Angel of Death is about to pass by all the houses in Egypt, to strike down the first-born of every family. This is the tenth and final plague. What actually saves the Jews is the sign on the outside of their houses. A sign that bears an uncanny resemblance to a . . . cross.

> *"Then they are to take some of the blood and put it on the sides and tops of the doorframes of the houses where they eat the lambs . . . The blood will be a sign for you on the houses where you are; and when I see the blood, I will pass over you. No destructive plague will touch you when I strike Egypt."*
> (Exodus 12:7, 13)

It is the evening and Nisan 14th has become Nisan 15th and Jesus hangs on a Roman cross, bloodied and dead. I simply have no time for detailed theology of the redemptive power of the cross and the forgiveness of sins. We must take this as a given. His shed blood has saved us, just as the blood of the lamb on the doorframes of the Jews saved them from death.

> *"In him we have redemption through his blood, the forgiveness of sins, in accordance with the riches of God's grace."*
> (Ephesians 1:7)

So Nisan 15th is a date anchored in history. Passover was the saving of the first-born Jews through the blood of the lamb and the Crucifixion was the saving of mankind through the blood of the Lamb of God.

> *" . . . For Christ, our Passover lamb, has been sacrificed."*
> (1 Corinthians 5:7)

Of course, as with Palm Sunday – thanks to the decision of the early Church to cut away from its Jewish roots – Easter is rarely celebrated on the correct day. In fact the name itself has no biblical significance, coming from *Eastre*, the ancient pagan goddess of the dawn. But that's another story!

But the story does not end there because that night Pharaoh relented and allowed the Hebrews in Egypt to leave *en masse*. This was the *Exodus* and well over a million souls marched out, celebrating their freedom from slavery.

So the Exodus began on Nisan 15th and it is commemorated by a second festival, the *Feast of Unleavened Bread*, which, for all intents and purposes, is generally seen as part of the Passover celebration. This festival, when only unleavened bread (Matzah), bread without yeast, may be eaten, lasts until Nisan 22nd.

> *"Celebrate the Feast of Unleavened Bread, because it was on this very day that I brought your divisions out of Egypt. Celebrate this day as a lasting ordinance for the generations to come."*
> (Exodus 12:17)

Unleavened bread plays a key role in the Passover service. It was certainly important for God because there were firm penalties for not eating it during this seven-day period.

> *"And whoever eats anything with yeast in it must be cut off from the community of Israel."*
> (Exodus 12:19)

What is all this about yeast? God makes it clear that yeast is a symbol of sin in our life.

> *"Therefore let us keep the Festival, not with the old yeast, the yeast of malice and wickedness, but with bread without yeast, the bread of sincerity and truth."*
> (1 Corinthians 5:8)

During the Passover service as it is conducted today, the unleavened bread provides us with an interesting picture, one that we already take on board every time we take part in Holy

Communion. In this rite we eat the "bread", which in the context of the Last Supper, really needs to be *unleavened* and is another example of how some Christian practices owe more to tradition than to biblical principles and practices. Consider this the next time you take your communion bread – unleavened bread represents sinlessness, it has holes (Zechariah 12:10) and stripes (Isaiah 53:5 KJV) and, during the Passover service, it is broken, wrapped in a linen shroud, hidden (buried), then found again (resurrected). You can have your Easter eggs, bunnies and bonnets, in terms of meaning and symbolism I'll take the *matzah* any day! Food for thought, eh . . . literally!

Biblical festivals also have an agricultural element and there's a third festival that runs in parallel with the others, starting on Nisan 17th. It is called *Firstfruits* and it signifies the beginning of the harvest.

> *"The LORD said to Moses, Speak to the Israelites and say to them: 'When you enter the land I am going to give you and you reap its harvest, bring to the priest a sheaf of the first grain you harvest.'"*
> (Leviticus 23:9–10)

Of course living as we do today, divorced from the sources of life's necessities, the provision of food from the ground has no significance other than price hikes in our local supermarket after a bad harvest, or difficulties with the food importer. But to many communities today and certainly to those living in biblical times, the barley and wheat harvest is extremely significant to their daily lives. Firstfruits is concerned with the barley harvest, but there's a spiritual significance too, because Nisan 17th was the day of Jesus' resurrection. Paul even makes the connection in his letter to the Corinthians.

> *"But Christ has indeed been raised from the dead, the firstfruits of those who have fallen asleep."*
> (1 Corinthians 15:20)

Knowing this gives us an insight into Paul's mind when he wrote it, bearing in mind his background as a learned orthodox Jew. He would have known that Jesus was resurrected just as the firstfruit wave offering was being made in the Temple and would have seen the prophetic significance. In fact it wasn't just the same day, but the same *hour* of the day. Jesus rose from the dead probably around sunrise, just as the high priest entered the Kidron valley, east of Jerusalem to harvest the first grain of the season, as a symbolic act. Just as the barley harvest was the first harvest, Jesus's victory over death was also the first of *all who have fallen asleep.*

Back to the Exodus. The Jews, led by Moses, streamed out of Egypt. We should know the story of the parting of the Red Sea and the provisions in the wilderness. The next big event was going to seal them together as a nation and the days were being counted . . .

The countdown started on the second day of Passover, near the start of the long march eastwards. For the Jews leaving Egypt it is going to be seven weeks before they reach Mount Sinai. This period of time is known as the *omer* and it takes us from the barley harvest to the grain harvest. The countdown ends at the next major Jewish festival, *Shavuot*, also called the Feast of Weeks. Christians know it as Pentecost. Interestingly the linking factor between these names is the number seven, the biblically "perfect" number. *Shavuot* means "weeks" and, of course a week has seven days. Pentecost means "the fiftieth day", which is derived from counting these seven weeks, inclusively.

> *"Count off seven weeks from the time you begin to put the sickle to the standing corn. Then celebrate the Feast of Weeks to the LORD your God by giving a freewill offering in proportion to the blessings the LORD your God has given you."*
> (Deuteronomy 16:9–10)

3 . . . 2 . . . 1 . . . blast-off. We are at Sinai, it is Shavuot and we are in a new month, Sivan, though, curiously, not on a fixed day.

Shavuot is always seen in relative terms, as the day that is seven weeks after Passover. The clue is in the name. It's strange if you think about it, a festival, classed as one of the big three in the Jewish year (the other two being Pesach – Passover – and Sukkot) having a name that is fundamentally meaningless. To give meaning to it, the Rabbis just counted the days and worked out what historical event came seven weeks after Passover . . .

While the impatient and unruly ex-slaves, stood around fidgeting, Moses climbed the mountain for a one-to-one with God Himself, receiving God's instructions for life and the Ten Commandments, inscribed by the finger of God on stone tablets. This was Shavuot and Moses was to spend 40 days and nights in the presence of God.

Shavuot became the *Time of the Giving of our Torah*. It celebrated the giving of the Torah, the teachings. In synagogues today it is not just the account in the Book of Exodus that is read out, but there are also readings from the Book of Ruth. There are intriguing connections. The story of Ruth also has an agricultural setting, at harvest time, but there's a spiritual connection too. Gentile Ruth's acceptance of the faith of Boaz the Israelite is seen as a parallel to the Children of Israel's acceptance of the covenant of God at Mount Sinai.

Now for something curious. Let us read what it says in Leviticus 23, in the instructions for subsequent generations to celebrate Shavuot.

"From wherever you live, bring two loaves made of two-tenths of an ephah of fine flour, baked with yeast, as a wave offering of firstfruits to the Lord.*"*
(Leviticus 23:17)

We already heard that *leaven* symbolises sin, a bad thing and that the Feast of Unleavened Bread drove that point home. But here we are, 50 days later, at Shavuot and the first thing we do is offer two *leaven* loaves to God.

An interpretation has been given, but not from Rabbinic Jewish sources and not explicitly biblical, so I can't pretend that any great authority is assumed. But it's a neat idea so I will mention it. The two leaven loaves are to represent sinful mankind, Jew and Gentile, two distinct groups but one single offering. It is a picture of our "One New Man".

> " . . . *by abolishing in his flesh the law with its commandments and regulations. His purpose was to create in himself one new man out of the two, thus making peace.*"
> (Ephesians 2:15)

So what have Gentiles got to do with Shavuot? Well, nothing directly but, after all, Shavuot was the time when *the Church was born.*

It is AD 33 (approximately, though some would say earlier) and Jerusalem is jam packed and overflowing with people. They are there because it is festival season, one of the three times a year that pilgrimages are made to Jerusalem. It is Shavuot, in this context you know it better as Pentecost and the Book of Acts tells us of the drama that ensued at that particular time.

> "*When the day of Pentecost came, they were all together in one place. Suddenly a sound like the blowing of a violent wind came from heaven and filled the whole house where they were sitting. They saw what seemed to be tongues of fire that separated and came to rest on each of them. All of them were filled with the Holy Spirit and began to speak in other tongues as the Spirit enabled them. Now there were staying in Jerusalem God-fearing Jews from every nation under heaven.*"
> (Acts 2:1–5)

On that day, as a result of the preaching of Simon Peter, three thousand Jews were ushered into the Kingdom of God. So, for believers in Jesus, Shavuot has two themes, commemorating two birthdays, the Law at Sinai and the coming of the Holy Spirit at Jerusalem. No ordinary day, this one!

Shavuot brings to a close the spring festivals of the Bible. As you have seen, as well as celebrating the harvest and telling the story of the Exodus and the birth of the nation of Israel, they illustrate and teach us about the redemptive acts of Jesus and the birth of the Church. They tell a biblical story in a way that the festivals of the Christian calendar never can. In contrast, Easter, with its pagan origin and moveable schedule, is bound by traditions divorced from the Bible and Pentecost is so stripped from its Jewish context that it may as well have landed from outer space.

We move into the summer months of Tammuz and Av. It's holiday time, the sun's out (in the northern hemisphere) and, certainly in the Land of Israel, it's hot, hot, hot.

In terms of agriculture, Bible history and the prophetic, it's a time of silence, waiting, inactivity. It's a time of lazing on the beach, reading a pulp novel, resting before the recommencing of the busyness. Rabbis use the summer months to recharge their spiritual batteries. It's the time of Moses and the Children of Israel, moaning and wandering around in circles in the desert. No real progress is made, but, although the days are not significant, the clock is still ticking. All is quiet on the Western Front and, then . . .

Returning to the Children of Israel, waiting for Moses at the foot of Sinai, for them it is hotter, hotter, hotter. You see, Moses was still up the mountain with God. He may have climbed the mountain at Shavuot, but remember he was to be in God's presence for forty days and nights receiving the Ten Commandments and finer points of the Law. Eventually he came down and . . . oh dear!

Now Jews are not known for their patience and the people waiting all those days at the foot of the mountain distract themselves by building a golden calf and offering sacrifices to it. God is most displeased and offers to blot them out and start building up a new people from Moses' family. Moses does not take up this offer and reminds God of the great investment He has made in these people, urging Him to continue with the line of Abraham, Isaac and Jacob. These are verses worth re-reading for those who believe that prayer can't change situations!

Having broken the stone tablets of the Law in disgust at this behaviour, Moses was to *schlep* up Mount Sinai for another forty days and nights. Meanwhile, back to the future (or our present) . . .

The silence of the summer months is shattered by a loud trumpet sound. It's not a shiny engineered brass trumpet, but rather a twisty, ungainly and whiffy ram's horn, the *shofar*. It's still hot, the end of summer, but the mood has changed. Paperbacks are discarded, beaches are deserted and navels are examined. It's the beginning of the time of introspection, a forty day period, a kind of Jewish *Lent*, the first thirty days taking over the whole month of *Elul*. These forty days, according to tradition, coincide with Moses' second trip up Mount Sinai, for the second set of stone tablets.

Not a happy month, the shofar is blown every morning and the theme is repent! Repent! Repent, before it is too late! This is the season of repentance, or return to the Lord, *teshuvah*. You've got thirty days to get right with the Lord. The Jewish sage, Maimonides, gives four steps to achieving this – *Stop* what you're doing if it's a wrong action, *have regret* for doing it, *verbalise* this regret to God, then *make a plan*, to make sure it doesn't happen again. So, that's the theme for the month and it is paramount that a good job is made of it because a day is coming . . .

On the first day of the next month, Tishrei, that day arrives. It is the Feast of Trumpets (*Yom Teruah*), also known as the Head of the Year (*Rosh Hashanah*), also known as the Day of Judgement (*Yom HaDin*). It is the Day of the Awakening Blast. The shofar blows extra hard this day, at least a hundred times during a typical synagogue service, so if that doesn't wake you up, you are already dead! Leviticus talks about this day.

> *"The* Lord *said to Moses, 'Say to the Israelites: "On the first day of the seventh month you are to have a day of rest, a sacred assembly commemorated with trumpet blasts. Do no regular work, but present an offering made to the* Lord *by fire."'"*
> (Leviticus 23:23–25)

Two things are suggested, both surprising. Firstly, God tells the Jewish people to rest, gather together, blow the shofar and offer sacrifices. So this they do, a couple of million Israelites milling around in the desert, shofars being blown throughout the camp and the great plumes of smoke rising to the sky with the smell of charred flesh. The shofar stops, then silence as all look to Moses and a single voice asks, "What's the deal here, Moses?" You see, the Bible never actually says *why* we have the Feast of Trumpets! Everything that is associated with this feast, apart from the blowing of the shofar, comes to us from Jewish tradition. Which brings me to the second point.

No. *Rosh Hashanah* is not the New Year, biblically speaking. As already said, the name means "head of the year", it is also called the "birthday of the world". Tradition tells us that God created the world on this day, hence you can see how it came to be known as New Year's day. In fact it's known as the civic, or secular, New Year and Jewish calendars mark this fact but, as the verse above shows, it is the first day of the *seventh* month, Tishrei.

New Year's Day in our calendar is a time of celebration, starting in the pubs and clubs on the night before and usually completed by a long lie-in or invigorating walk in the country-side. Rosh Hashanah, by way of contrast, offers nothing to celebrate. For a start, we are still in the period of navel-gazing, teshuvah, and decision time has been reached – not by any human beings but by God Himself. If you are a righteous Jew He writes your name in the Book of Life and if you're a wicked Jew, your name goes into the Book of Death. As it is unclear who these people are, at least to the people themselves (the wicked being in denial and the righteous being too modest to call themselves so), most (in fact all of them, if you think about it) go into neither book. This is because God, according to tradition, gives folk one last chance, over the next ten days, the *Days of Awe*, to repent before it is too late! Synagogues go into overdrive during this period to remind their (hopefully) trembling flock to sort themselves out before it is too late.

These ten days, in fact the whole period of teshuvah, end at *Yom Kippur*, the Day of Atonement. The name tells it all.

> *"The* LORD *said to Moses, 'The tenth day of this seventh month is the Day of Atonement. Hold a sacred assembly and deny yourselves, and present an offering made to the* LORD *by fire. Do no work on that day, because it is the Day of Atonement, when atonement is made for you before the* LORD *your God. Anyone who does not deny himself on that day must be cut off from his people. I will destroy from among his people anyone who does any work on that day. You shall do no work at all. This is to be a lasting ordinance for the generations to come, wherever you live. It is a sabbath of rest for you, and you must deny yourselves. From the evening of the ninth day of the month until the following evening you are to observe your sabbath.'"*
> (Leviticus 23:26–32)

It's the most solemn day in the biblical calendar, the holiest day in the Jewish year. For the Jew it's the real day of reckoning, it's the end of the Days of Awe, when you find out if you have made the grade, hit the mark, earmarked for Death or Life. In biblical times, when the Temple in Jerusalem still stood, the High Priest would make the annual sacrifice for the people of Israel. *Yom Kippur* literally means the "day of covering", in the sense of your sins being covered, or pardoned, at least for a while. This was the only way ancient Jews could be reconciled to God for their sins until Jesus came along and showed a better way, *the guarantee of a better covenant* (Hebrews 7:22).

When the Temple was destroyed in AD 70, sacrifices could no longer be offered and, outside salvation offered by the death and resurrection of Jesus, there was no way back to God. So instead the rabbis and sages instituted a system of good works to get back into God's good books, a man-made tradition that's still with us, in the form of the anxiety of *are we righteous enough to get into the Book of Life?*

At the end of this solemn day, with the final blast of the shofar, according to Jewish tradition the gates of heaven that had opened on Rosh Hashanah are now closed, your fate sealed and unknown unless you have the misfortune to come knocking at the gates during the forthcoming year (i.e. you've died)! To complete our link with the past, it was also said to be this day when Moses descended Mount Sinai for the second time, with brand new stone tablets.

A question you are asking. What have these two autumn festivals got to do with Christians living today? First a short recap. We have followed the events from Egypt to Sinai, spanning Passover to the Day of Atonement on the biblical calendar. We also saw how the final events in the life of Jesus took us from Passover to Shavuot and how these spring festivals form the context for the death and resurrection of Jesus and the birth of the Church. But what about the autumn festivals? What do they tell us about Jesus? Actually quite a lot . . . in a prophetic sense.

Prophetically, the autumn festivals speak to us not of the life and death of Jesus, but His return, the *Second Coming*. Although messianic theologians agree in principle that this is so, the actual timetable of events is heavily dependent on your view of the end times, regarding such contentious issues as the *rapture*. Here is the general gist of it, starting with a scripture.

"Listen, I tell you a mystery: We will not all sleep, but we will all be changed – in a flash, in the twinkling of an eye, at the last trumpet. For the trumpet will sound, the dead will be raised imperishable, and we will be changed."
(1 Corinthians 15:51–52)

The last trumpet, the last trump, the last shofar. Another name for Rosh Hashanah is *Yom Teru'ah*, the Feast of Trumpets, so there's a connection here. The Talmud tells us that on this day the dead will be raised (Rosh Hashanah 16b), so Jewish and Christian expectations are identical. It is reasonable to assume that, if there is to be a rapture of the Church, Rosh Hashanah is a fair bet for that actual day, but I'm not going to second-guess our God, who tells us that it is not up to us to know such things.

> *"No one knows about that day or hour, not even the angels in heaven, nor the Son, but only the Father."*
> (Matthew 24:36)

So it could just as easily be on April 24th, February 9th or July 1st. Who knows? Who cares? Just be *wise virgins* and be prepared . . . always!

Yom Kippur also has prophetic significance. It is associated with that great and terrible day, the *Day of the Lord*, or the *Day of Judgement*.

> *"The sun will be turned to darkness and the moon to blood before the coming of the great and glorious day of the Lord."*
> (Acts 2:20)

On this day will come the blowing of the Great Trumpet, *Shofar HaGodal*, and Jesus Christ will return to Earth, the *Second Coming*. As I said earlier, although it will enrich our walk with the Lord if we view these events in a prophetic sense rather than a literal sense, otherwise we may end up one of those poor folk who spend these holy days up the top of some mountain, in order to be the first to be swept heavenwards when Jesus returns!

There is one more biblical feast in the Jewish calendar, perhaps, in the context of this book, the most relevant one of all. It is the Feast of Tabernacles, *Sukkot*, the Feast of Booths. It is the seventh and last of the biblical feasts and it is celebrated between the 15th and 22nd of Tishri, just a few days after Yom Kippur.

> *"So beginning with the fifteenth day of the seventh month, after you have gathered the crops of the land, celebrate the festival to the LORD for seven days; the first day is a day of rest, and the eighth day also is a day of rest. On the first day you are to take choice fruit from the trees, and palm fronds, leafy branches and poplars, and rejoice before the LORD your God for seven days. Celebrate this as a festival to the LORD for seven days each year. This is to be a lasting ordinance for the generations to come; celebrate it in the seventh month. Live in booths for seven days: All native-born Israelites are to live in booths so your descendants will know that I had the Israelites live in booths when I brought them out of Egypt. I am the LORD your God."*
> (Leviticus 23:39–43)

As with the other agricultural festivals (Passover and Shavuot), it can be looked at in a few different ways. Originally, it was the Feast of Ingathering, as instructed to Moses on Sinai.

> *"Celebrate the Feast of Ingathering at the end of the year, when you gather in your crops from the field."*
> (Exodus 23:16)

Then, as the Leviticus passage shows us, it is a memorial to the Children of Israel, wandering through the desert for forty years. It is called the Feast of *Booths* because the people lived in booths, temporary shelters, as they meandered on their journeys.

Then there is the Jesus connection, both looking back and looking forwards, which is what makes this feast most interesting. Looking back, here are three episodes in the life of Jesus that illustrate this.

> *"The Word became flesh and made his dwelling among us. We have seen his glory, the glory of the One and Only, who came from the Father, full of grace and truth."*
> (John 1:14)

Many Bible scholars have looked at this passage and realised that the Greek words translated as "made his dwelling" also take the meaning "tabernacled". So Jesus was born on this Earth and *tabernacled* with us. They investigated further and began gathering biblical evidence, particularly from the account of Zechariah, father of John the Baptist, ministering in the Temple (Luke 1:5). It says that he belonged to the priestly division of Abijah and research indicates that this would have been during the period from Sivan 12th to 18th. Knowing that John the Baptist was conceived at that time and adding on nine months, we arrive at John's birth around Passover time. Knowing that Jesus was conceived six months after John's conception, we get the birth of Jesus, six months after Passover . . . around the Feast of Tabernacles! Suddenly John 1:14 makes sense and the Christmas industry start gunning for Hebrew scholars!

Sacred cows sacrificed at the altar of truth! Who said Jesus was born on December 25th anyway? It was a date of convenience, manufactured by the early Roman Church to cause minimum disruption to the pagan society that had suddenly become a "Christian" one! Of course any proposal to change this date to a more meaningful one is not going to be met with meekness, but I will make a suggestion on this a little later on.

Jesus made a trip to Jerusalem to celebrate Sukkot.

"On the last and greatest day of the Feast, Jesus stood and said in a loud voice, 'If anyone is thirsty, let him come to me and drink. Whoever believes in me, as the Scripture has said, streams of living water will flow from within him.'"
(John 7:37–38)

This last and greatest day is *Hoshana Rabbah*. When you consider that this is translated as "the Great Salvation" and that the people in Jesus' day would circle the altar seven times, declaring "Save now!", you see the significance of Jesus' utterance. He was referring specifically to the water drawing ceremony but speaking of the living water of the Holy Spirit, soon to be poured out for all mankind.

Moving to the beginning of Jesus' final week on Earth we come to the curious event of his Triumphal Entry into Jerusalem. Why curious? Well, read on . . .

> *"Many people spread their cloaks on the road, while others spread branches they had cut in the fields. Those who went ahead and those who followed shouted,*
>> *'Hosanna!'*
>> *'Blessed is he who comes in the name of the Lord!'*
>> *'Blessed is the coming kingdom of our father David!'*
>> *'Hosanna in the highest!'"*
>
> (Mark 11:8–10)

It is curious because, although this all happened at Passover time, all the symbolism of their actions was *Feast of Tabernacles*. The words spoken, the spreading of the branches, are all connected to this festival. So what happened, was there a mass delusion and confusion over dates?

No, their actions were prophetic because Sukkot was believed to be the festival most associated with the start of the Messiah's reign on Earth. Here's where we read about this.

> *"Then the survivors from all the nations that have attacked Jerusalem will go up year after year to worship the King, the Lᴏʀᴅ Almighty, and to celebrate the Feast of Tabernacles. If any of the peoples of the earth do not go up to Jerusalem to worship the King, the Lᴏʀᴅ Almighty, they will have no rain."*
>
> (Zechariah 14:16–17)

Another name for Sukkot is the "Feast of the Nations" and this is where we look forwards in time, by looking back to this prophecy in Zechariah. These events have not yet happened, Jesus is not yet ruling the Earth from Jerusalem. But there's an

important point to make here. God is speaking here and He is
telling us that, at some future date, the nations, Gentiles and
Jews together, will have to set aside one time to visit Jesus in
Jerusalem. When is this time – Easter, Christmas, Whitsun? No
it's at a time that our current Church has neglected, it's at a
Feast of the Lord that has been rejected by the Church and only
kept alive by the Jewish people. How on Earth are the Nations
going to be able to avoid drought and pay homage to the King
of kings if they don't know when to book their flights and what
they should be doing when they get there? Is this not proof
enough of the importance of an understanding of the biblical
festivals of the Lord?

Although we started our biblical year in spring and we are
just in autumn, the key biblical feasts have run their course.
There are other minor festivals, some of them biblical, some
traditional, some civic, and they all tell a story. Unfortunately
we do not have the room to tell their story here. But our seven
main festivals – Passover, the Feast of Unleavened Bread,
Firstfruits, Shavuot (Pentecost), Trumpets, the Day of Atonement and the Feast of Tabernacles – all tell a consistent story
on three different levels. Firstly, they mark out the seasons,
reminding us of God's provisions for us in season. Then they
lead us through the narrative of Moses and the Exodus, leading
us from captivity in Egypt to the formation of a nation on the
way to the Promised Land, being helped and guided by God
every step of the way.

Thirdly, this whole process also has a parallel in the Christian
life. *Coming out of Egypt* is also a biblical metaphor for leaving
behind the old godless life and we can follow every stage of the
story in Exodus and pause in wonder at how God leads us
through our own personal Exodus when we become a Christian.
The blood on the doorposts is the saving blood of Jesus, cross-
ing the Red Sea is our statement of faith through water baptism,
the pillars of cloud and fire are the Holy Spirit guiding our
journey, living (or tabernacling) in us, just as the Children of

Israel lived in temporary booths in the wilderness. There is so much more, we have just scraped the surface, believe me – the Old Testament narratives and the story of the biblical festivals have such depth, all we need is the time to learn and study more – I can see another book coming on here . . .

Then, of course, we see Jesus . . . everywhere. Every one of the seven feasts tells us something about Him, about His life, death and subsequent career. The spring feasts speak of His mission on Earth and the autumn feasts tell us of His mission from Heaven. All part of the same story, except that the final autumn events have not yet happened.

So we have the January to December calendar, named after Roman pagan gods and loosely ordered by Christian traditions. Then we have the Nisan to Adar calendar, curiously named after Babylonian pagan gods (why oh why couldn't we have had something like – Abruary, Isaacary, Jake . . . etc.), but at least tightly ordered by biblical events. What do we do next? Am I proposing the dumping of the Western calendar and going biblical? Do we jettison everything that is forged at the altar of tradition as unbiblical? Do we all become grinches at Christmas? Do we shoot the Easter bunny and serve up rabbit at the Passover meal?

The solution is actually simple. As Christians there is only one festival, or sacramental act, that we are obliged to take part in and that is the Lord's Supper. Jesus said,

"Do this in remembrance of me."

He never actually told us to do anything else in remembrance of either Himself or any biblical event, in the Old or the New Testament. If this is all we do then that's fine. But of course we all like to get together on special occasions and so we should celebrate the festivals of the Lord. We don't have to celebrate them, we are not commanded to celebrate them. It is simply about blessing. All who partake in these festivals will be blessed in their understanding of Jesus and will also have the opportunity to better understand their Jewish neighbours and friends. But more of that later.

The Jewish festivals, the *biblical* festivals, are so instructional, so rich in meaning, so bursting in Jesus, that it can do us nothing but good to be aware of them, at the very least. It is totally up to you. Personally Christmas has gone full circle. It started off as a Roman pagan festival, marked by debauchery, over-indulgence and revelry and that's how it has ended up. I say leave it at that, by all means meet with family and friends and give presents, but don't bring Jesus into it. Yes, I've said it! I've spoken what is unspeakable in many circles. If you feel a need to celebrate the Nativity then perhaps sing your carols at the Feast of Tabernacles, but it really isn't any concern of Jesus' so perhaps it shouldn't be ours either.

Having said that, the last impression you would want to give to those family and friends who are not quite on the same path as yours, is of one of those kill-joy, humourless religious nuts who seeks to drain life out of everything that surrounds them. Whatever you decide it would be worth heeding the principle behind these words of Paul.

> *"So whether you eat or drink or whatever you do, do it all for the glory of God. Do not cause anyone to stumble, whether Jews, Greeks or the church of God – even as I try to please everybody in every way. For I am not seeking my own good but the good of many, so that they may be saved."* (1 Corinthians 10:31–33)

Be real, be sensitive to others, be joyful.

There's No Place Like Home

Jewish life through the ages has been bittersweet. The bitterness has been from without, the sweetness from within. Their communities have always lived in a precarious state, never accepted by the Christian world that surrounded them. Yet once the outside world had been shut out, life for ordinary Jews within their own communities had been a million times more meaningful, wholesome and joyful than that of their Christian neighbours. How ironic was that?

Let's first look at the dry facts. Christian Europe, for the few hundred years since Constantine declared Christianity as the official state religion, was such a disgrace that we label this period the *Dark Ages*. It was a time of continuous fighting, of superstition, of illiteracy, of poor health and general grief and sorrow. Yet this was meant to be the dawn of Christian civilisation, a secularised kingdom of priests but, when Rome fell, everything went to pot.

Although there were numerous historical processes at play, much of the blame for this can be placed on our usual suspect, Plato. Augustine wrote a book, *The City of God*, which, in the true spirit of Platonism, virtually wrote off life on Earth as unimportant. For him, life in an earthly city should never be a main concern for Christians, instead we should all aspire to the heavenly city, the City of God. Although he stated that our society should be based upon Christian principles, this never came to pass and the inequalities, injustices and deprivations of Christian Europe were excused as unimportant because *it will all be alright when we go to heaven.*

So while the Christian was living in poverty, ignorance and subservience, kept in place by the promises of the "next world", what of his Jewish neighbour? Let us consider the home. The Jewish home was always intended as a holy place. The Tabernacle in the desert and the Temple in Jerusalem in biblical times were holy places. They were known as a *miqdash*, meaning "sanctuary", a place set apart for worship of God. When the Temple was destroyed by the Romans, the rabbis declared that every Jewish home should become a holy place, referring to them as a *miqdash me'at*, a "small sanctuary". The home was to be a place for worshipping God, a holy place. Tradition tells us that, when the Temple was destroyed, the *shekinah*, God's Glory, didn't settle in the synagogues, where you would have expected it to, but made its home in every Jewish home. God was truly identifying with the people where they lived. Isn't this a profound yet wonderful thought? While the Christians at that time trapped God in cold, busy, glitzy cathedrals and churches, as the exclusive property of the clergy, with visiting rights granted to the *hoi polloi* every Sunday, in Jewish tradition God was present in the place where they slept, ate and gathered together as families.

Whereas in Christian tradition, the focus for activities is the Church building, for the Jew it is the family home. The home is to be a "house of prayer" for the worship of God. It is to be a "house of study", for the learning of God's Word. It is also to be a "house of assembly", a place where people are welcomed. Added to that it is also to be a "house of eating and drinking", a "house of sleeping", a "house of making love" and so on. Try doing that lot in Church, see how far that gets you!

Most Christians travel to Church every Sunday and watch

as the priest/minister/pastor/vicar conducts various spiritual rituals on their behalf, from administering Holy Communion to the hymn/prayer sandwich, to the thirty minute sermon. Religious Jews, by contrast, are told to "know God in all your ways", which involves every aspect of their lives. Think about religious occasions. Where do Christians celebrate Christmas and Easter? They go to Church, at least for the "religious" aspects, the rituals and the liturgy. Where do Jews typically celebrate their religious occasions? In their home. For example, for Jews since biblical times, Passover is a tightly structured occasion that is firmly anchored in the home environment, from the hunt for *chametz* (leavened bread), which requires a complete cleaning of the home prior to the festival, to the welcoming of strangers to partake of the meal with the family. In the Feast of Tabernacles, *Sukkot*, temporary shelters are built adjoining the home, where at least one meal is eaten and some (in hotter climes than ours) even attempt to sleep in them.

Even the everyday act of eating is celebrated with spiritual connotations. The dinner table corresponds to the altar of the Temple. Does that mean they worship food, an accusation often directed at Jewish people? No, because even eating is a sacred act and the dinner table will also function as a place where words of godly wisdom are exchanged in the conversations that accompany the eating, where Hebrew prayers resound and songs are sung in praise of their God.

Then there is the Sabbath, the *Shabbat*, celebrated from Friday sundown to Saturday sundown.

> "*If you keep your feet from breaking the Sabbath*
>   *and from doing as you please on my holy day,*
> *if you call the Sabbath a delight*
>   *and the* Lord's *holy day honorable,*
> *and if you honor it by not going your own way*
>   *and not doing as you please or speaking idle words,*

then you will find your joy in the LORD,
 and I will cause you to ride on the heights of the land
 and to feast on the inheritance of your father Jacob.'
    The mouth of the LORD has spoken."
(Isaiah 58:13–14)

The principle behind it is simple. God rested on the seventh day after creating the Heavens and the Earth, and so should we. Of course the goalposts have been moved now, and, following Jesus' lead, the Sabbath is not obligatory for Christians.

"Then he said to them, 'The Sabbath was made for man, not man for the Sabbath.'"
(Mark 2:27)

But this is not the point. The fact is that this most important of all Jewish holidays (Holy Days), as Jesus reminded us, was meant for mankind, for joy, for rest, for family fellowship. Unfortunately, at times, it had become dry ritual and encumbered by volumes of rules and regulations. At the time of Jesus, thousands of these had been created, listing what you can and can't do on this day, surely substituting the joy and the freedom with added unwelcome regimentation.

For religious Jews now, Sabbath is a time for family and friends, a time to pray, to sing songs, to read, to rest from the frantic business of the rest of the week. One thing they don't do is work and thirty-nine categories of forbidden tasks have been created to remind them of what they can and can't do on this day. Here they are, without commentary.

Carrying, burning, extinguishing, finishing, writing, erasing, cooking, washing, sewing, tearing, knotting, untying, shaping, ploughing, planting, reaping, harvesting, threshing, winnowing, selecting, sifting, grinding, kneading, combing, spinning, dying, chain stitching, warping, weaving, unravelling, building, demolishing, trapping, shearing, slaughtering, skinning, tanning, smoothing and marking.

Is anything left? It seems an impossible task to keep Sabbath but human beings are by nature adaptable and a Jewish Sabbath lifestyle is perhaps made special by its very difference from the norm. Through these restrictions, the day itself becomes detached from the rest of the week and consequently stands out as a day put aside for God.

For a Christian, the *Sabbath*, has been moved to a Sunday. It is regarded as the day you go to church, but, apart from that obligation, generally the secular world has chipped away at Sunday and, in most ways, it has lost much of its specialness and has even become a working day for many (including the clergy, of course!). Perhaps the rules and regulations of the Jewish Sabbath have been more of a blessing than people realise? Perhaps Jews need them for their own good, to keep creeping secularism at bay, to preserve an oasis of holiness away from the pressures and demands of the outside world.

Just compare the two days. There is little special any more about the Christian Sunday "Sabbath". Is it really a day of joy, rest and family fellowship, or is it just another day for work, shopping or the frantic search for entertainment? Yet the Jewish Sabbath, celebrated at the centre of religious life, the Jewish home, has generally successfully cut off the outside world and provided a day that is certainly different from every other day.

A home is where you can be real, where you are *you*. If we considered our homes in the same way as religious Jews then there would be no room for hypocrisy. We could hardly be "Sunday Christians", wearing our "Sunday best" and reserving our pious religious face for those Sunday moments, then undoing our belt and resuming our bickering with our spouse in the car on the way home! Instead our home becomes our church and God has His beady big eye on us 24/7. Can we handle that? In a way that's irrelevant, as God has His beady eye on us anyway, whether in our homes or in our church and whether we like it or not. It's all a matter of perception really. And if our home is our church, is it "open all hours", do we welcome the stranger, are our pews available for all?

Where there's a home, there are people. Of course, people don't always get along with each other, least of all families, but in the home of the religious Jew there is a standard set, *shalom bayit*, a peaceful home, that is worth striving for. It is an aspect of that most overused Hebrew word (along with hallelujah and amen), *shalom*. The usual understanding is that of peace, either internally as a calmness or externally as an absence of war. Shalom is a six-lettered word with tons of meaning. In its truest sense it invades all areas of mind, body and spirit. It implies health, safety, completeness and wholeness. In Israel it is used both to greet people and say goodbye. It's an all-purpose word – when confronted by a Jew, when in doubt, just wish them shalom and you've made a start.

So *shalom bayit*, peace in the home, is important, particularly as the Jewish home is such a hub for the family and community. Its truest expression is defined by the core of every family, that sacred covenant between two people known as marriage. To achieve shalom bayit one needs to achieve domestic bliss, so you've got to get your relationship right with your spouse first. This brings us to the marriage covenant itself.

The Jewish marriage covenant is a wonderful thing indeed, not just in the practical sense, but in what it teaches us about God, Israel and the Church. I will now take you through the steps of the Jewish wedding ceremony and we will not only see the spiritual principles behind the physical rituals but we will examine wider principles that take us right to the heart of what God means by "covenant".

It all starts with courtship, or you may need the services of the *schadchen* (matchmaker), depending on time, cost or degrees of attractiveness. Then it's time to meet the parents and haggle over the price. This is the *bride price*, the amount the man is willing to pay his prospective in-laws for his wife to be. This was all part of the betrothal process which involved a contract being drawn up, the *ketubah*, the marriage contract.

Both God and Jesus had marriage contracts drawn up, according to the Bible. God had one drawn up with the Kingdoms of Israel and Judah and the contract was, in fact, the book of Deuteronomy!

> *"'The time is coming,' declares the* LORD,
> *'when I will make a new covenant*
> *with the house of Israel*
> *and with the house of Judah.*
> *It will not be like the covenant*
> *I made with their forefathers*
> *when I took them by the hand*
> *to lead them out of Egypt,*
> *because they broke my covenant,*
> ***though I was a husband to them,'***
> *declares the* LORD.*"*
> (Jeremiah 31:31–32, emphasis added)

But the Northern Kingdom of Israel broke the terms of the contract, by committing spiritual adultery, and was summarily divorced and sent packing.

> *"I gave faithless Israel her certificate of divorce and sent her away because of all her adulteries."*
> (Jeremiah 3:8)

The southern kingdom of Judah also committed adultery but was spared from divorce, on account of promises made to King David and the necessity of ensuring an unbroken messianic line, leading to the birth of Jesus generations afterwards.

*"Nevertheless, for the sake of his servant David, the L*ORD *was not willing to destroy Judah. He had promised to maintain a lamp for David and his descendants forever."*
(2 Kings 8:19)

Jesus Himself had a marriage covenant drawn up with the Church. The first mention of it is in the passage in Jeremiah already mentioned.

*"'The time is coming,' declares the L*ORD,
'when I will make a new covenant
with the house of Israel
and with the house of Judah.'"
(Jeremiah 31:31)

This is the New Covenant made with the house of Israel and the house of Judah. Yes, you heard it right. The New Covenant, the new marriage contract drawn up by God, was with the whole house of Israel. This may surprise some people, but here it is in the Bible, the only time it is explicitly mentioned. The New Covenant, as detailed in the words of the New Testament, was, in the first instance, with Israel. Of course Gentiles were eventually allowed in too and all those who accepted the terms of this covenant also became the people of God, the Church.

So the first marriage, between God and Israel, failed on account of the bride's adultery. The second marriage is to be between God's Son and the Church, both Jew and Gentile. No wonder the Church has had a problem with the Jews – no-one gets on with their mother-in-law do they (think about it)!? Joking aside, there's a lot we can learn from this new marriage covenant, between Jesus and the Church.

The first thing to note is that the wedding hasn't yet happened. We are still at the betrothal stage, the Church is just *engaged* to be married to Jesus. He proposed to us during the Last Supper when He said:

"Then he took the cup, gave thanks and offered it to them, saying, 'Drink from it, all of you. This is my blood of the covenant, which is poured out for many for the forgiveness of sins.'"
(Matthew 26:27–28)

This covenant was to be made possible by the shedding of Jesus' blood as the sacrifice for sin. He paid the bride price with His life. Our acceptance of this covenant is dependent on our response to this act. In the act of betrothal it is Jewish custom to share a cup of wine together, so we can see the connection here. When we take Holy Communion it is a reminder of our betrothal to Jesus. We are partakers in the longest engagement period in history!

Another Jewish custom at the time of betrothal is for the groom to present his bride with special gifts, mementos to sustain her during the engagement period. The Bride of Jesus, the Bride of Christ, the Church has received the greatest gift of all, that of the Holy Spirit.

"Peter replied, 'Repent and be baptized, every one of you, in the name of Jesus Christ for the forgiveness of your sins. And you will receive the gift of the Holy Spirit.'"
(Acts 2:38)

"But the Counsellor, the Holy Spirit, whom the Father will send in my name, will teach you all things and will remind you of everything I have said to you."
(John 14:26)

What a gift, what a reminder! A very practical gift indeed!

Also, during this period the groom has to prepare a place for them to stay in after the wedding, the wedding chamber. This is usually built in his father's house, to his father's specifications.

Jesus also spoke of this to His bride, the Church. So a place is being prepared for Christians to stay with Him immediately after the Wedding ceremony.

> *"Do not let your hearts be troubled. Trust in God; trust also in me. In my Father's house are many rooms; if it were not so, I would have told you. I am going there to prepare a place for you. And if I go and prepare a place for you, I will come back and take you to be with me that you also may be where I am."*
> (John 14:1–3)

During the betrothal period, the couple is considered as husband and wife. This is shown in the following passage.

> *"This is how the birth of Jesus Christ came about: His mother Mary was pledged to be married to Joseph, but before they came together, she was found to be with child through the Holy Spirit. Because Joseph **her husband** was a righteous man and did not want to expose her to public disgrace, he had in mind to divorce her quietly."*
> (Matthew 1:18–19, emphasis added)

Sex was prohibited during this period, which is why the sudden and inexplicable pregnancy of Mary was a public disgrace and Joseph quietly planned to divorce her.

> *"But after he had considered this, an angel of the Lord appeared to him in a dream and said, 'Joseph son of David, do not be afraid to take Mary home as your wife, because what is conceived in her is from the Holy Spirit.'"*
> (Matthew 1:20)

Until he was shown the complete picture, of course.

Returning to the Bride of Christ, the engagement can't last forever. Eventually the moment must come, the marriage ceremony, the wedding. One day the wedding chamber will be ready and the groom's father signals the all-clear, now fetch your bride! The shofar is blown and the groom comes for his bride.

Wow, those of you into end-times stuff would immediately see the connection here. Because there will be a time when Jesus comes back for his bride, the Bride of Christ, the Church.

> *"For the Lord himself will come down from heaven, with a loud command, with the voice of the archangel and with the trumpet call of God, and the dead in Christ will rise first. After that, we who are still alive and are left will be caught up together with them in the clouds to meet the Lord in the air. And so we will be with the Lord forever."*
>
> (1 Thessalonians 4:16–17)

The next fact you can take or leave, but it's the next item in the Jewish wedding narrative. In the ceremony, the newly weds will spend seven days in the wedding chamber, then the groom presents the bride to the world, a sort of second coming, or Second Coming, for those with a dramatic bent! Then comes the wedding supper, or Wedding Supper. You can build your own prophetic interpretations around this, I am certainly not getting drawn into end-times speculation!

> *"Then I heard what sounded like a great multitude, like the roar of rushing waters and like loud peals of thunder, shouting:*
>
> *'Hallelujah!*
>   *For our Lord God Almighty reigns.*
> *Let us rejoice and be glad*
>   *and give him glory!*
> *For the wedding of the Lamb has come,*
>   *and his bride has made herself ready.*
> *Fine linen, bright and clean,*
>   *was given her to wear.'*
>
> *(Fine linen stands for the righteous acts of the saints.)*

> Then the angel said to me, 'Write: "Blessed are those who are invited
> to the wedding supper of the Lamb!" And he added, "These are the true
> words of God."'"
>
> (Revelation 19:6–9)

Back to the Jewish home. Although the marriage covenant is
the starting point, the natural consequence is the building up
of a family. The Jewish family unit has been the bedrock of their
culture and a key factor to the incredible survival of the Jewish
people. While mayhem ruled around and about, this God-
ordained unit ticked away doing its stuff, feeding, nurturing
and educating the next generation. For example, the Passover
ceremony is primarily geared towards teaching the children and
reminding them of their heritage.

As you enter a religious Jewish home the first thing you notice
is the small object affixed to the door post. This is the *mezuzah*,
a box containing a scroll. On the scroll are the following verses
from the Bible.

> "Hear, O Israel: The Lord our God, the Lord is one. Love the Lord your
> God with all your heart and with all your soul and with all your strength.
> These commandments that I give you today are to be upon your hearts.
> Impress them on your children. Talk about them when you sit at home and
> when you walk along the road, when you lie down and when you get up.
> Tie them as symbols on your hands and bind them on your foreheads.
> Write them on the doorframes of your houses and on your gates."
>
> (Deuteronomy 6:4–9)

This defines everything. It is the *Shema*, the most revered Jewish
prayer. It declares the centrality of God and His commandments
in this home and the necessity of passing on these beliefs to the
children of the household.

The Hebrew word for family is *mishpochah*. The key concept
here is that it is not the nuclear family of 2.4 children that we
have been brought up with, but the extended family that includes

grandparents, uncles, aunts and cousins, where the cooking pot is in permanent use, where the atmosphere jangles with human voices, cries, prayers and laughter, where caring and sharing crosses the generations. This has become an utterly alien concept to most of us these days. We strive for our own space, we crave personal expression. Community has been replaced by individuality as we disengage our lives from people and replace them with stuff, such as consumer electronics, furniture and objets d'art. Stuff doesn't answer back, stuff doesn't have demands, stuff doesn't need looking after.

But stuff doesn't look after you when you're poorly, stuff doesn't go that extra mile for you, stuff doesn't love you. Mishpochah ensures that the wisdom and stories of your grandparents are not lost, mishpochah celebrates family occasions as extended times of joy and sharing, mishpochah provides an endless supply of babysitters, household operatives and shoulders to cry on. Mishpochah means you never need to be lonely, though it could also potentially be stifling and claustrophobic. Mishpochah, though, does require a big house.

Central to the whole concept of home and family in the Jewish world is the need to teach the next generation.

"These commandments that I give you today are to be upon your hearts. Impress them on your children."
(Deuteronomy 6:6–7)

The centre of religious life, as I said earlier, is the home not the synagogue. In fact the Hebrew word for parent, *horeh*, has the same root as *moreh* and *torah*. The latter two words mean "teacher" and "teaching", so a primary role of a Jewish parent is as a teacher. Traditionally the three roles of a Jewish father are to support his family, study the Bible (Torah) and see that his children study the Bible.

The rabbis tell us that *the world is poised on the breath of schoolchildren* and the education of Jewish children was always seen as an absolute priority. The Talmud (Mishnah Avot 5:21) tells us what sort of education these kids would have received, at the time of Jesus. It started at the age of five, when Bible training started, first from the Book of Leviticus, to understand the rituals and then from the Psalms, to understand the nature of God. At the age of ten, study began on the Oral Law and at the age of thirteen one was old enough to fulfil the laws and commandments. At fifteen they learned the works of the sages. By this age Holy Scripture was as familiar to them as the history and characters of our favourite soap, or line-ups of our sports teams are to us. To be fair, they weren't burdened with the distractions we have now, with the internet, TV, radio, satellite and cable, magazines, paperback books and so on. But, then again, we're not exactly *forced* into filling our heads with nonsense and trivia.

Despite living in the most deprived, precarious conditions, Jewish communities in Christian Europe never sank to the lows of those who surrounded them. Their communities flourished where possible because of the strength of the family unit and the centrality of the home in all aspects of their lives. They lived lives of wholeness in mind, body and spirit, guided by the Hebrew Scriptures and the wisdom of the rabbis. It wasn't an easy life, or even a particularly happy one, but they did the best that they could, secure in their perception that God was with them, despite the sorry state they found themselves in. The relationship between the Jew and his God has always been an interesting one and it is where we shall go next.

CHAPTER 10

Our Father God

This is our God.

> "Then the man [Adam] and his wife [Eve] heard the sound of the LORD
> God as he was walking in the garden in the cool of the day, and they hid
> from the LORD God among the trees of the garden. But the LORD God called
> to the man, 'Where are you?'
>
> He answered, 'I heard you in the garden, and I was afraid because I
> was naked; so I hid.'"
>
> (Genesis 3:8–10)

> "'Do not come any closer,' God said. 'Take off your sandals, for the place
> where you are standing is holy ground.' Then he said, 'I am the God of
> your father, the God of Abraham, the God of Isaac and the God of Jacob.'
> At this, Moses hid his face, because he was afraid to look at God."
>
> (Exodus 3:5–6)

This is our God. Scared? You should be! The trouble is, we're
not and we really really should be. Yes, God is more approach-
able than He seemed to be in Old Testament times, but He's
no pussycat. Quoting from the *Narnia* books, Aslan is *not a
tame lion.*

Many Christians today seem to have lost the real sense of
awe and reverence for our holy God. Remember, He is the same

yesterday, today and forever. The same God who met with Adam
and Moses, who terrified them with His presence, is the one
who supposedly has casual chats and loses arguments with
certain modern-day "prophets" and "apostles".

Some high profile TV preachers and teachers seem to have
such a special relationship with the Almighty God, Creator of
the Heavens and the Earth, that they are able to twist Him
around their little fingers, get Him to change His mind about
the most trivial of items, force His will through perceived loop-
holes. They do this to reinforce that most Greek of ideas – them
and us, clergy and laity, anointed and commoners. They believe
that they are God's special anointed, specially selected people
with divine channels of communications, little Popes with big
ideas, giving them licence to take almighty liberties.

Believe me God has no special relationship with self-styled
Super-Christians, God's Dread army, His Generals, Manifest
Sons of God, or whatever else many of them may call themselves. If God has lowered Himself to the degree that He has
become a partner in such shenanigans then we all might as well
pack up and go home and flush our membership cards down
the toilet! Harsh words indeed, but I worship a God who will
not be manipulated and twisted and treated like a playground
chum. I follow an awesome God who destroyed wicked nations,
who saw off Ananias for cheating on a property deal, who rained
down burning sulphur on Sodom and Gomorrah. My God is
not a tame lion!

Yet God is a personal God and if we didn't believe that prayer
changes things then surely we wouldn't bother. He is intensely
interested in our comings and goings and cares deeply about
us. The Sodom and Gomorrah episode shows us God having
His mind changed by Abraham.

> *"Then Abraham approached him and said: 'Will you sweep away the*
> *righteous with the wicked? What if there are fifty righteous people in*
> *the city? Will you really sweep it away and not spare the place for the*

sake of the fifty righteous people in it? Far be it from you to do such a
thing – to kill the righteous with the wicked, treating the righteous and
the wicked alike. Far be it from you! Will not the Judge of all the earth
do right?'
  The LORD *said, 'If I find fifty righteous people in the city of Sodom,*
I will spare the whole place for their sake.' "
(Genesis 18:23–26)

Yes God does listen to us and can change His mind. But there's
a chasm the size of a small planet between Abraham's pleadings
for the life of the righteous and a TV preacher commanding
God to authorise a thousand-fold increase for those who send
in their hard-earned cash. If religious Jews had their own TV
station there would be none of this nonsense (though probably
replaced with other different types of nonsense!). Why am I so
certain? Well it's all down to the Jewish view of God.

The start point is the prayer that is in the mezuzah that Jewish
families attach to their door-posts. It is the *Shema*, the most
important prayer in Judaism and the bedrock of their understanding of God.

"Hear, O Israel: The LORD *our God, the* LORD *is one. Love the* LORD *your*
God with all your heart and with all your soul and with all your strength."
(Deuteronomy 6:4)

This prayer is recited by religious Jews every morning and
evening and more so on Sabbath and festivals. For many Jewish
martyrs, from the time of the Maccabees to the Holocaust, it
is the last thing uttered before death.

It very simply defines who God is and how we should treat
Him. There is just one God and our duty is to love Him with
all parts of our being. It is a command, which implies that if it
doesn't come natural to us, then we must work on it. It is a
command, just like the Ten Commandments, that ask us not
to murder, steal, commit adultery, covet or lie – all things that

are part of our basic fallen nature. We must work on the idea of loving God, just as Jesus asks us to love our enemies. Jews are commanded to love God even though He is ultimately responsible for the sorry state that they find themselves in, as a generally misunderstood and hated people.

It has to be said that these days much of the Church seems to follow a different God, a touchy-feely God of their own expectations and desires, a God crafted out of their own imaginations, a God that makes them feel good and feeds their self-esteem. We need to search for the real God, not an imaginary one. But how do we know if we have found Him? Just look for a Father's heart. No sermon here, but just think of the characteristics of a loving father, offering tough love not fluffy love and start praying and searching.

There is a song in the Jewish liturgy that expresses this idea perfectly, *Avinu Malkeinu*, our Father, our King.

> *"Our Father, our King, we have no king beside You. Our Father, our King, for Your own sake have mercy on us!"*

To Jews it illustrates what is called the *immanence-transcendence paradox*. How God, the Creator and Ruler of the Universe, can also offer the intimacy of a loving father. Christians, of course, have no problems with this, but tend to veer to the opposite extreme in outlook. The popular view of God for most Christians is as a Father in Heaven. The popular view of God for religious Jews is expressed in the first few words of their daily prayers over food, wine etc.

> Blessed are you, Lord our God, *King of the Universe* . . .

Jews have a problem with His intimacy, many Christians have a problem with His majesty. There's much that each can teach the other. So what can Jewish thoughts and practices teach us?

Firstly, due to the inherited Greek mindset, early Christians had tended to overanalyse the things of God. We read earlier of the doctrine wars of the Early Church, brought about by the subtle influence of Greek philosophy. It is worth repeating what was earlier stated: the Greek mind says that we should strive for knowledge *about* God, the Hebrew mind says that we should *know* God. You can see Him shouting from the heavenlies, STOP READING ABOUT ME, ARGUING ABOUT ME . . . JUST TALK TO ME AND GET TO KNOW ME!

To be honest, these days this has been a problem more so for Jews, than for Christians. What it shows us is that even religious Jews need to rediscover their own Hebrew mind-set, even they have succumbed to the influence of the Greeks. The Hebrew mindset tells us that, although doctrine is crucially important, just as important is a *relationship* with God. These days most Christians are rediscovering this, the problem has been taking it too far, when relationship has given way to *familiarity*. There is no such problem with religious Jews, as we shall now see.

How many times do you hear the three lettered word, *God*, these days? First there's the popular usage, in blind ignorance of the Third Commandment.

> *"You shall not misuse the name of the LORD your God, for the LORD will not hold anyone guiltless who misuses his name."*
> (Exodus 20:7)

"Oh my God!", "God help me" and their ilk can be heard in offices, homes and schools throughout the nations. God calls this blasphemy and there are consequences for such flippancies, so be warned. The other place where this word is heard, in more reverent terms, is in Church of course, in Bible readings, prayers, sermons, liturgy and worship songs. One place you'll never hear this word (or read it) is in a synagogue or in a religious Jewish home. Yes, you may say, *it's because they use the Hebrew word for it, you're trying to trick me!*

No, religious Jews have such a reverence for God that they can't even write or say His name. When a scribe was copying Scripture onto a new scroll and came across the name of God, he had to use a special quill to write this most holy of names. In conversation these days, when referring to Him they use the word *HaShem*, which simply means "The Name". They take the Third Commandment seriously! When they need to write His name down they miss out the vowel and write either G–d or L–rd. It is a practical reverence and, to be honest, for some it is borderline superstitious, but the intention is sincere.

Whenever reading from the Bible or prayer books, religious Jews also have another rule regarding the Name of God. In Hebrew script, the actual Name of God, as written by Moses and the other compilers of the Bible, has four letters, all consonants, as there are no vowels in biblical Hebrew. Whenever Jews read this word, the word that they actually say is "Lord", rather than saying the name of God and opening themselves up to the possible breaking of the Third Commandment. How this actually works is described later on in this book, when we examine the Hebrew language.

So, what have we learned? We must take our G–d seriously, very seriously. Here are a few reminders.

"For the LORD *your G–d is G–d of gods and Lord of lords, the great G–d, mighty and awesome, who shows no partiality and accepts no bribes."*
(Deuteronomy 10:17)

"Speak to the entire assembly of Israel and say to them: 'Be holy because I, the LORD *your G–d, am holy.'"*
(Leviticus 19:2)

"The voice of the LORD *is over the waters;*
  the G–d of glory thunders,
  the LORD *thunders over the mighty waters."*
(Psalm 29:3)

This is our G–d, the G–d of Jews and Christians, of the Old Testament and New Testament. The same G–d then, now and forever. He doesn't change, we don't change, but what did change was the way that He communicates and deals with us. These verses in Jeremiah remind us of this.

> *"'This is the covenant I will make with the house of Israel*
>   *after that time,' declares the* LORD.
> *'I will put my law in their minds*
>   *and write it on their hearts.*
> *I will be their God,*
>   *and they will be my people.*
> *No longer will a man teach his neighbour,*
>   *or a man his brother, saying, "Know the* LORD,*"*
> *because they will all know me,*
>   *from the least of them to the greatest,'*
>   *declares the* LORD.
> *'For I will forgive their wickedness*
>   *and will remember their sins no more.'"*
> (Jeremiah 31:33–34)

These verses spoke of awesome things, the new way that God was going to communicate with His people. God was going to move from the Holy Places of the Jews to the holy place within each and every Jew who allows Him to, from the Temple in Jerusalem to the temple of the body. He is going to become a more personal God in this New Covenant, *putting His law in their minds and writing it on their hearts.*

So although our God is now a personal God, it doesn't mean we can take liberties with Him. He is still the God of the *Shema*, the God known reverently and respectfully as G–d, whose name is never spoken of directly and who is just known as *HaShem*, The Name.

The Greek mind says that we should strive for knowledge about God, the Hebrew mind says that we should know God.

The Hebrew understanding of God is one of reverence and respect. It is of acceptance of His majesty and greatness and seeks to please Him, for no other reason than He is the Creator of the Heavens and the Earth. The Greek mind is not completely satisfied by this and wants to know how God ticks. It seeks to know the unknowable, understand the un-understandable (that's a new word!). To the Greek mind, the intellect must be exercised, even if this exercise is futile. This is why there have been wars over doctrine. They haven't been wars about God Himself, but about competing understandings of the Father, the Son and the Holy Spirit.

The Jews of the Old Testament fought their wars either as instructed by God or in defiance of Him. Victory depended on which of these options they took. If they acknowledged God and did what He asked, then He gave them victory in battle.

> *"For the* LORD *your God is the one who goes with you to fight for you against your enemies to give you victory."*
> (Deuteronomy 20:4)

Christians of the medieval Church era and onwards fought their wars not over God Himself, but over interpretations of their beliefs in God. They were doctrine wars, not holy wars.

Christians, it is time for us to get real with our God, our Creator and our Father.

Redoing Religion

The dry definition of Religion is: *a belief in and reverence for a supernatural power or powers regarded as creator and governor of the universe.* Filling in the blanks that defines Christianity as: *a belief in and reverence for God, the Creator and King of the Universe.* The question I now ask is, if we follow such a Big God why do we cram Him into such a small box? We should let Him loose, let Him roam freely, let Him act according to His awesome nature. Of course He already does, but we act as if He lived just in ancient buildings, sports halls on a Sunday hire, or in front rooms swept clean of profane literature and embarrassing relatives. The Bible gives us a more realistic view of God:

> *"Where can I go from your Spirit?*
> *Where can I flee from your presence?*
> *If I go up to the heavens, you are there;*
> *if I make my bed in the depths, you are there.*
> *If I rise on the wings of the dawn,*
> *if I settle on the far side of the sea,*
> *even there your hand will guide me,*
> *your right hand will hold me fast.*
>
> *If I say, 'Surely the darkness will hide me*
> *and the light become night around me,'*

even the darkness will not be dark to you;
   the night will shine like the day,
   for darkness is as light to you."
(Psalm 139: 7–12)

There's no escape. God doesn't just live in church buildings for a couple of hours every Sunday. He is everywhere and there is no escape from His presence. He is present with the astronaut in the space station and with the coal miner deep underground. He would even be with us in the darkness of our minds, the place where many of us conceive the most shameful acts.

How we *do church* is in many ways a product of Greek thinking rather than biblical instruction. For a start, nowhere in the Bible is *Church* ever meant to be a building. It was always referred to as a group of Christians. It was the Greek Church Fathers who changed things, leading to an idea that any expression of Christianity is best confined to a meeting place rather than the people who meet there. Whereas Jesus tells us to go out into the world and preach His Gospel, we have ended up telling the world to come into Church, to find Jesus there. And what does the world really find when it goes there?

First, the building. For those of you who meet in house churches, sports halls or modern ecclesiastical edifices, this is not for you, so you are absolved in advance. For the rest of you, it may be a surprise for you to know that church buildings were originally based on Roman government buildings, which were in turn based on Greek pagan temples. The man chiefly responsible for the prominence of church buildings was our old friend, Emperor Constantine. He gave the people no choice, passing a Law prohibiting Christians from meeting anywhere other than in a Catholic Church. This meant that folk couldn't meet in homes or public arenas and it cemented State control for the official religion of the state. It was very similar to what we see today in China, with their measures against Christians meeting in "house churches".

And the churches that were built were for a particular purpose. Constantine's choice of design was to provide an environment where the masses could be seated most efficiently to passively watch a performance.

Here was the *dualism* of Plato in action, the separation of the clergy (up front doing the stuff on a raised platform) and the laity (the commoners watching the performance from behind a screen). The original churches were also built facing east, so that, as with Greek Temples to the Sun god, the sun shone around the face of the speaker. There was little distinction between the Son of God and the sun god in many minds.

In the centre of the original church building was the altar, the most holy place. The whole idea of the altar was both from the Jewish Old Testament and the Christian New Testament. In the Old Testament it was the place of sacrifice in the Temple in Jerusalem. In the New Testament we have the *eucharist*, the bread and the wine for Holy Communion, which was placed on the altar in the church. This was considered such a holy act that only the clergy could administer it. Again we see more Platonism, forbidding ordinary (physical) folk to take part in "spiritual" duties, which is certainly not the intention, as described in the Gospels. *"Do this in remembrance of me"*, Jesus told His disciples, the first-century equivalents of you and me. It was meant to be a simple memorial performed by ordinary Christians, not administered by special people in robes.

Also "holy relics" of dead "saints" were stored beneath the altar, a pagan practice and a corruption of the verse in Revelation, which speaks of heavenly matters.

"When he opened the fifth seal, I saw under the altar the souls of those who had been slain because of the word of God and the testimony they had maintained."
(Revelation 6:9)

The whole idea of the altar has absolutely no place in the Christian faith. Our bodies are the temple of God, an idea that Plato would have had no truck with, of course – the spiritual living inside the physical, oy vey!? The altar is no more as the Temple in Jerusalem is no more. Christ has made the ultimate and far-reaching sacrifice once and for all, so who needs an altar?

What else do we see in the church building? I've never liked the word *pew*. It's a puny, effete little word, a tiny pursing of the lips and out it comes. It's a clever device to pack in a large group of people into a small space and to give the illusion of sacrifice by making the experience quite uncomfortable and restrictive. It has turned the Christian experience into a spectator sport, reinforcing the divide between clergy and laity. The clergy do their stuff on the stage at the front and the pew dwellers watch the performance, only interacting when directed by the performers.

This is a model that is still with us and has many faces. It has allowed us to emulate the world and provides us with "celebrity" preachers, teachers, prophets and apostles who, when churches are not big enough, draw in the crowds to sports stadiums, conference centres and tents and to television sets around the world. This is not a criticism of these people, as they are purely functioning within the parameters of this age, thoroughly Greek parameters in this case.

This got me thinking. The secular model for presenting an entertainment to a large group is now firmly established. Picture the scene. A large stadium filled to capacity with excited fans, facing a raised platform packed with multimedia paraphernalia for sound amplification and TV broadcasting, huge plasma screens on both sides of the stage. The band starts up, guitars, keyboards, drums slice through the atmosphere with a steady crescendo of sound, a rhythmic cadence to some, a wall of noise to others. The MC stumbles to the microphone and announces the star, who arrives from the side to rapturous applause. The preacher has arrived!

This is where we are. This could be a Coldplay concert or it could be a worship service, same difference except for the message. When we have arrived at a situation where the latest Christian worship leaders dress the same as their secular counterparts, share the same musical genre and sound levels as their secular counterparts and follow the same stagecraft, then we begin to wonder if the blurring at the edges is a smokescreen to choke us to death. Watching a so-called "outpouring" live on my TV, I asked myself if those in the stadium, warmed up by an hour of high volume rock music with repetitive rhythmic patterns, simplistic lyrics, slogans and shouting, were really encountering a revival experience, or were psychological influences setting the agenda? *Was this true worship?* I asked myself. Was God boogieing away in heavenly places? Were the angels swaying to the throbbing bass beat? *What is true worship?* I ask myself now.

Going from the general to specific, we start with the accepted definition, as *reverent love and devotion to one's God.* This is fine, but the key question is *how we worship?* The Greek word for *worship* in the New Testament has the sense of "falling down before" or "serving" God.

> "On coming to the house, they saw the child with his mother Mary, and they bowed down and worshiped him. Then they opened their treasures and presented him with gifts of gold and of incense and of myrrh."
> (Matthew 2:11)

So this is our response to our mighty God, a voluntary sense of giving ourselves to Him. *Shachah*, the Hebrew word for worship, in the Old Testament also has the sense of bowing down or prostrating ourselves to God.

> "Ezra praised the LORD, the great God; and all the people lifted their hands and responded, 'Amen! Amen!' Then they bowed down and worshiped the LORD with their faces to the ground."
> (Nehemiah 8:6)

Being pedantic, then, a true act of worship in the biblical sense is to prostrate oneself before God in adoration. So when a worship leader tells us that we are now going to worship God, why do we stand up to sing a song rather than fall to the ground? What has happened to our understanding of worshipping God?

Now for a surprise. Worship is not just about music, or praise, or prayer. Many Jews have believed that *study of God's Word* is the highest form of worship. Studying the Torah is considered an act of submission to God's will, a sincere attempt at understanding Him better, so that they could be better people. A Greek view of study is to gain understanding for understanding's sake, so that philosophers can spend endless hours arguing over some miniscule aspect of doctrine, an intellectual locking of horns. Wars have been fought over such mind games. This is not worship. It does not necessarily draw us closer to Him.

A Hebrew view of study would be to get to know God and His ways just a little bit better, so that this knowledge can be put to practical use. This is a form of worship as it is a genuine acknowledgement of God and a reverence for Him. Jews have always been a people of brain rather than brawn, unless there are giants to fell with a slingshot or a country to defend. Jewish heroes have been eggheads rather than jocks.

Of course study is not the only way that religious Jews worship God. Prayer is paramount, of course. But it's not necessarily prayer that is familiar to Christians, in both content and delivery. To see corporate prayer in action in the Jewish world, visit the Western (Wailing) Wall in Jerusalem during the Sabbath. It's a cacophony, with each individual Jew crying out to God, in full ritual garb and movement, with deep swaying from the hips. This is not holy exercise, it is the act of *davenning*, and it rocks . . . to and fro . . . literally! Jewish prayer often includes a lot of movement and can be summed up quite adequately by Psalm 150.

"Praise the LORD.

Praise God in his sanctuary;
  praise him in his mighty heavens.
Praise him for his acts of power;
  praise him for his surpassing greatness.
Praise him with the sounding of the trumpet,
  praise him with the harp and lyre,
praise him with tambourine and dancing,
  praise him with the strings and flute,
praise him with the clash of cymbals,
  praise him with resounding cymbals.

Let everything that has breath praise the LORD.

Praise the LORD. "

To the Jewish mind, God is to be worshipped at all times, not just at the appointed times. As mentioned in an earlier Chapter, there are prayers for just about everything, all detailed in the prayer book, the *Siddur*. Prayers for eating, drinking, even snacking. Prayers for going to sleep and for waking up. Prayers for emptying bowels and for washing hands. Even prayers for good news, bad news and special occasions.

These prayers are typically short and share the same structure. These are known as blessings, *berakhot* and typically begin with the following words:

Barukh atah Adonai, Eloheinu, Melech haOlam
Blessed are you, Lord our God, King of the Universe

This pattern affirms at all times, who is being prayed to and reminds us of His awesomeness. Hey, we're not chatting to a mate here, we are thanking, worshipping, blessing the divine Person who brought us all into existence, breathed life into the human race and sustains us daily according to His grace and mercy. It is always worth getting these things into perspective and reminding ourselves of the sheer privilege of not just being alive, but being chosen as one of God's special children, a Christian.

Another expression of our worship is through dance. There is one form of Jewish dance that has made great inroads into churches in recent years and that is *Davidic dance*, patterned on Israeli folk dances and taking its name from King David, who *danced before the Lord* (2 Samuel 6). These are not just dances for royalty, but are typically group dances for people of all sexes, ages and dancing prowess. The dances can range from the slow and devotional to the exuberantly joyful.

> *"Let them praise his name with dancing*
>   *and make music to him with tambourine and harp."*
> (Psalm 149:3)

To a religious Jew everything is spiritual, everything is theological, everything is sacred. Life is not compartmentalised. By now you have probably got my drift and can now understand this key distinction between the Greek thinking that has insinuated itself into all parts of Church thinking and practice and Hebrew thinking that has been waiting in the wings for far too long!

Jesus once had a spat with a Samaritan woman about acceptable ways to worship God. He spoke to her of a future time.

> *"Yet a time is coming and has now come when the true worshipers will worship the Father in spirit and truth, for they are the kind of worshipers the Father seeks. God is spirit, and his worshipers must worship in spirit and in truth."*
> (John 4:23–24)

So worship is going to have to be infused in spirit and truth. It needs to be of a spiritual nature because God is spirit, but it needs to be based on truth.

The use of memorised songs as the predominant form of worship has come about historically as a result of the high degree of illiteracy in earlier times. People didn't read much, if at all. Hymns were how many people got their theology, so it has always been important that they contained sound doctrine, based on the truth of God's Word. Of course we are more literate these days, though not always Bible-literate. Worship songs are all well and good and helpful, but are no longer necessary to fulfil the role as the main channel of doctrine to the masses. Yet many people still do get their doctrine from our worship songs. Perhaps it is now time to free oneself from the past and break free and explore other ways to worship God, other ways to feed oneself from the Word of God, like reading the Bible!

The big point to make is that the Western Church has evolved (or devolved) into a rigid pattern whereby the phrase "we will now move into a time of worship" is a cue for throats to be cleared, brains emptied of the mundane and legs and arms placed on standby and "praise and worship" is understood as a musical genre. This is Greek understanding, it puts God in a box and misrepresents Him as someone who can only be worshipped in recognised spiritual ways, such as prayer, singing and proclamation. Hebrew worship frees us up totally to worship Him using every part of our created being, body and soul, with our arms, legs, voice, mind and spirit. God created every part of us, so every part of us has been divinely cleared for take-off! How this theory can be put into practice will be covered in the final chapter of this book.

It's a shame that there is so little literature around that can tell us more about the *original* Church, so that we can learn more on how they did things. I am not referring to the Church of Constantine, or even that of the Church Fathers, but the Jewish Church which is mentioned, with not too much detail, in the Book of Acts. Luke, the writer of the book, was writing a history and focused, unsurprisingly on the *acts* of these first Christians, the Acts of the Apostles. Maybe one day we'll find a companion volume, the *Lifestyle of the Apostles*, detailing *how* they worshipped God and "did Church", but until then, we're feeding from scraps!

The problem is that most writings by early Jewish believers (apart from the apostles, of course) were destroyed by the Gentile Church, deemed heretical (too Jewish) by their theologians. In other words, these Jewish writings were either canonical or diabolical! Most information we have on the Jewish Church was written by Church historians, who were not going to be very sympathetic in their treatment. History has tended to be written by the victors! The one thing that we can discern was that those early believers were meeting both in homes and synagogues. Even Gentile converts were meeting with their Jewish brethren in synagogues and observing the Jewish Sabbath and festivals, at least until the Church edicts were passed banning them from doing so.

There are some clues though, in the pages of the New Testament, particularly in the Book of Acts. Here is one of them, regarding Paul and his attitude on the Jewish festivals. In Acts 20, we read of him hurrying to get back to Jerusalem to celebrate Shavuot (Pentecost), so obviously it still meant something to him.

"Paul had decided to sail past Ephesus to avoid spending time in the province of Asia, for he was in a hurry to reach Jerusalem, if possible, by the day of Pentecost."
(Acts 20:16)

For these first believers, many of them had the advantage of actually meeting their Messiah in the flesh, or at least knowing of Him. For them, Christianity was a straightforward faith. It wasn't primarily defined by rules and regulations, it was about one person, Jesus. Belief in the person of Jesus and all that He did for us, has always been the key to faith. These days many Christians deny that they are following a religion, rather they are following a person, Jesus, but for the Church of Constantine and onwards, it wasn't that simple. It was all about doctrines, complexly worded philosophical statements, borne out of the Greek mind and which Christians argued over and fought over.

Remember, in the last section, we talked about the conflict between the Arian or the homoousian or the homoioousian positions, with regard to Jesus' position within the Godhead. This was the natural outcome of viewing Christianity as a philosophy rather than a pure faith. It just complicates what is really a simple faith in the life and death of Jesus Christ, no wonder the Western world plunged into the Dark Ages at this time!

So we have been given the opportunity to rediscover the Jewish ways of worship and understanding of doctrine, following in the footsteps of the first Christians. Part of this process is to look at the language that underpins it all, the language that defined their religious life. All is told in the next chapter.

God's Language Unravelled

12

Think of the word, *sin*. Just a three letter word, quite unfashionable, even among many Christians today. What does it make you think of? It's perceived as a negative word, best summarised by the numerous similes (or cop-outs) used as a substitute for it by trendy preachers or embarrassed Christians, words such as peccadillo, offense, transgression, failing, wrongdoing, crime or misdemeanour. But, what about the word itself, that vowel sandwich of a word? If you were meeting this word for the first time, would there be anything about the word itself, all three letters of it, that would give you an idea of its meaning? The answer is simple. It is a resounding "no". The English language doesn't offer such a service.

Hebrew is very different. It is a pictorial and evocative language, it speaks through its own structure. The usual Hebrew word for "sin" also has three letters (consonants actually) and transliterates as *chatha*. Its usual meaning is to "miss the mark". So a Jew living in biblical times would see this word and a picture would immediately form in his mind, of an arrow speeding towards a target, but never hitting it. A mundane word or idea has been used to express a spiritual concept. This is Hebrew thinking in action, bringing the spiritual down to Earth. By missing the mark, the idea is expressed that mortal man always seems to fall short of the mark that God sets for him. That is the idea of sin.

There are a few other Hebrew words used for "sin". Each of them provides a picture of their meaning. The word *'avah* is to be bent or crooked, *amal* evokes the idea of trouble and toil and *'avar* means to cross over, translated as a transgression. These words are all used in different circumstances in the Hebrew Scriptures, but always in the general context of "sin". The word used in each case would indicate a special subtlety in its use that would be picked up by the reader.

Another word that a little Hebrew knowledge can shed some light on, is *Torah*. This is a most misunderstood word by Christians today, who usually translate it as "law" or, should I say "LAW", the *unyielding, stifling, restrictive Old Testament concept that we are all thankfully free from now*. This is a complete nonsense and I will explain why. But, first, we need to know a little about biblical Hebrew root words.

The thing about Hebrew in the Bible is that it is basically a string of consonants, the vowels came many centuries later. So, unless the ancient Jews spoke in a guttural rasp, reminiscent of deconstructed Vulcan (a la *Star Trek*), which would have needed constant lubrication to avoid throat seizure, they would have added vowels and created words that would be totally alien to the modern Hebrew speaker. We know the consonants, as they were written down, but as the vowels have been lost, we can never be absolutely sure how to pronounce the words. So the Masoretes, the scholars who added the vowels in the fourth century AD and onwards, were basically just using guesswork!

That leaves us with just consonants, when we look at the original biblical Hebrew text. Scholars and sages have studied this text and conjured up the words out of this string of consonants, giving us the Old Testament we know and love. What they found is that most of these words are variations of a number of three letter *root words*, from which common meanings can be extracted. Basically, if you can gain an understanding of these root words, then the Hebrew Scriptures can really start to open up for you and the patterns of God's wisdom will instruct and delight you. Of course I am not speaking from experience here, I am no Hebrew scholar. We are fellow travellers on this particular path, my friend!

The word *Torah* comes from a three letter root word, *yarah* (remember, root words don't have vowels, so the actual word is *yrh*). This word means to throw something, or shoot something, like an arrow from a bow. It also alludes to a finger pointing something out. Another connected word is *moreh* (*mrh*), which refers to the person doing the throwing or shooting, or the person doing the pointing out. A moreh, in Hebrew understanding, could therefore be an archer shooting an arrow, or a teacher pointing out something. By slightly adjusting this root word (an acceptable practice in Hebrew, not a fudge!), we arrive at *torah* (*trh*), which is what is shot out by the archer, or what is taught by the teacher. In other words, we have an arrow or a teaching. So Torah can mean teaching and this is illustrated in this verse from Proverbs.

> *"My son, do not forget my* **teaching** *[torah],*
>   *but keep my commands in your heart."*
> (Proverbs 3:1, emphasis added)

But we can go further in our understanding here. Remember, the principle of the mundane illustrating the spiritual. Our word Torah also means an arrow shooting at a target. So here we have the sense of the Torah being a teaching that has a direction and a purpose. To fulfil the Torah is to "hit the target" or "hit the mark". *Wait a minute* (I hear you say) . . . *where have I heard this before?* Of course, we have already covered the Hebrew word, *chatha*, meaning "sin", which conjured up the picture of "missing the mark".

So this brief introduction to biblical Hebrew has given us a mental picture of the Torah, the instructions given by God through Moses to Israel, as arrows aimed at a target, representing God's direction for us. But these arrows are not always going to hit the target, because of the sin in the lives of the people.

Hebrew may be God's mother tongue, but it's an earthy language. As we have seen, it uses the mundane to express the spiritual. It employs all five senses when writing or reading or speaking or hearing. Here is an example.

"The LORD is compassionate and gracious,
slow to anger, abounding in love."
(Psalm 103:8)

Looking at this passage in Hebrew, the word translated as anger is *aph*. This literally means nose, or nostrils and the sense taken is that when one is angry the nostrils flare! So the literal translation is "slow to nose", but a picture is drawn, using a common everyday fact, of anger being expressed.

Let's now see what else biblical Hebrew can teach us in terms of our understanding of God Himself.

Remember when we learned earlier that religious Jews refuse to refer directly to God's name, but use the term *HaShem*, "The Name", instead? This is reverence for almighty God, but also tinged with fear because of the dire consequences associated in Jewish tradition for uttering the *actual name* of God, something that only the High Priest in the Temple in Jerusalem could utter. As he is no more, the name remains unuttered.

In the Hebrew Scriptures, which, as you know, is all consonants, whenever God is referred to in a personal manner, a word of four letters is used, YHWH. This is known as the *Tetragrammaton*, a Greek word meaning . . . four letters. This word appears well over six thousand times in the Old Testament, in every book except for Esther, Song of Songs and Ecclesiastes.

Now, what can a religious Jew do when he's reading from the Hebrew Scriptures and comes across this word – he can hardly avoid one of the thousands of times that it appears, after all. He has to say something, whether it's in his own mind or out aloud. What he does is substitute it for another word, *Adonai*, which means "Lord", usually written "LORD". The Masoretes, the Jewish scholars who added the vowels to the Hebrew Scriptures, actually added the vowels of the word Adonai to the consonants of the word YHWH, to remind the reader not to use the unutterable name, but to say Adonai instead.

So, in common speech, when a religious Jew wants to refer to God, he uses HaShem, but when reading the Bible or sacred literature, he uses Adonai. This is respect and reverence.

Christians generally have no such reverence for God's name and when they see the Tetragrammaton, YHWH, they prefer to have a go at pronouncing the word. So what did they do? They looked at the Hebrew text with vowels as produced by the Masoretes and noticed that YHWH had vowels. Not realising that these were not the *actual* vowels of God's name, but just a memory aid, they decided to pronounce what they saw. This is the origin of the word *Jehovah*. It's not God's name, it's a word created by man. In fact the man in question was Peter Galatin, Pope Leo X's confessor, in the sixteenth century.

The next time the Jehovah's Witnesses come a-knocking ask them who they are witnessing for, because it's not a God that is written about in the Bible! That should rile them. Others have used the word *Yahweh*, which is also wrong for the same reason. It's a lot safer and more respectful to use the word LORD, but at least if we use the word "God", as in this book, we know who we are talking about!

Although YHWH is God's sacred personal name, it's not the only way He is referred to in the Old Testament. The first time we meet Him in the Bible, a different name is used.

Bereshit bara Elohim et hashamayim ve'et ha'arets
In the beginning God created the heavens and the earth

The word here is *Elohim*, which appears well over 2,000 times in the Hebrew Scriptures. This is not His personal name, it's just the word, "God" and is a plural word, which is quite intriguing, alluding to the Trinity of course. The singular word for this is *Eloah*, which also appears in Scripture, mainly in the Book of Job. There's another word that's even smaller than this, *El*. This word is also used around 250 times in the Old Testament and is associated with power, might and strength. It is most often used in constructs, either as the start of a word or as the end of a word.

Many biblical characters have names that remind us of God, by having *el* tacked onto the end. Here are a few of them: Ezeki-el (God strengthens), Isra-el (Struggles with God), Gamali-el (Camel of God), Ishma-el (God that hears) and Emmanu-el (God is with us).

We can even look beyond the Bible to see these same principles hijacked by popular culture. *Is it a bird? Is it a plane? No, it's SuperMoses!* Did you know that the Superman character was created in the 1930s by two American Jews, Jerry Siegel and Joe Shuster as a response to the growth of anti-Semitism both in the USA and in Europe. They developed a very Jewish mythology around the character and gave him the name of *Kal-el*, and called his father *Jor-el*. It was Jor-el on the Planet Krypton who places his son in a tiny rocket ship in order to save him from the catastrophe to come.

That's enough of mere mortals (and super-mortals), now for some more names for God Himself.

> *"When Abram was ninety-nine years old, the LORD appeared to him and said, 'I am El-Shaddai (God Almighty) walk before me and be blameless.'"*
> (Genesis 17:1, emphasis added)

> *"Into your hands I commit my spirit;*
>   *redeem me, O LORD, El-Emet (the God of truth)."*
> (Psalm 31:5, emphasis added)

In the above two verses you can see how YHWH has been translated as Adonai, meaning LORD.

> *"Was it not I, the* Lord*?*
>   *And there is no God apart from me,*
> **El-Tsaddik** *(a righteous God) and a Saviour;*
>   *there is none but me."*
> (Isaiah 45:21, emphasis added)

In the above verse, the word Elohim has been translated as God. Let's see another verse now, first in English.

> *"He will receive blessing from the* Lord
>   *and vindication from God his Saviour."*
> (Psalm 24:5)

Now let's fill in a few gaps with Hebrew.

> *"He will receive blessing from* **Adonai**
>   *and vindication from* **Elohim** *his* **Yeshua***."*
> (Psalm 24:5, emphasis added)

You've spotted a new word and, if it's familiar to you, you are wondering what on Earth it is doing in the Old Testament! Picture the scene. It's two thousand years ago, in a small village called Nazareth, in the Galilee region of what is now the Land of Israel. You see a little boy playing in the backyard among the wood piles and shavings. His father, *Yosef*, is in the workshop next to the yard and his mother, *Miriam*, is busy cooking. His name is *Yeshua ben Yosef*. You know him better as Jesus, son of Joseph.

But what's Yeshua doing in the Old Testament?, *you ask.* Surely his "Old Testament name" is Immanuel (or Emmanuel)?

> *"Therefore the Lord himself will give you a sign: The virgin will be with child and will give birth to a son, and will call him Immanuel."*
> (Isaiah 7:14)

Immanuel (or Emmanuel) or Jesus? Which is it to be? The answer is . . . both! This is the beauty of Hebraic thought. Names are not just . . . names. Names are to have meaning. The Bible is full of this concept. Virtually everyone in the Bible has a name that describes something relevant about that person or the situation in which he or she found themselves. From Adam (Hebrew for "man") to Zechariah ("God has remembered") we have a cast of thousands of colourful characters. Then, of course, Jesus, with over 350 names, each describing an aspect of His nature or mission. The name *Yeshua* means "salvation". As He chiefly came to save the world, then surely it is apt that His given name reflects that fact. *Emmanuel*, as we have already seen and from what the Gospel account tells us, means "God with us", a comfort to us all, but still not a name with the power of *Jesus*, Our Saviour. We could call Him Emmanuel, Son of Man, Son of God, the Word or Messiah, but it's far more convenient to call Him by the name His mum and dad were told by an angel to give Him, Jesus, or *Yeshua* in Hebrew.

And so ends our introduction to the colourful world of biblical Hebrew. I would hope that you are intrigued enough to find out more, because a knowledge of the language of the Old Testament will surely open up the Scriptures in remarkable ways.

We have completed our vignettes of Hebraic thought and hopefully it has acted as a taster for you, an appetiser to encourage you to partake in many feasts to come. We are now about to move ahead in other ways, interesting ways . . .

PART THREE
Balance

" . . . His purpose was to create in himself
one new man out of the two, thus making peace."

(Ephesians 2:15)

One New Man Revisited

13

I have wrestled with the concept of "One New Man" for many years. A website, Saltshakers, that I co-founded around twelve years ago, has had the verse from Ephesians as its strap line, with a vague desire to see Jews and Gentiles in perfect, seamless, sincere fellowship. Oh what a naïve dreamer I was! The most visible initiatives in the Christian world to attain this dream have been Messianic fellowships and "One New Man" networks and, worthy though the intentions are, they still trouble me.

What I see is a reaction, a pent-up release after sixteen hundred years of frustration, injustice, persecution and, let's be frank, hellishness. In that period, the Jewish element wasn't just lost to the Church, but deliberately seared away with white-hot tongs. A sixteen century travesty is hard to forgive and forget just like that. So what we get is a reaction. A reaction by Jewish believers who look to break away from the hurtful past and create something new, outside the established Church, fuelling liturgy, beliefs and practice in a thoroughly Hebraic way but having little to do with the rest of the Body of Christ. *Don't call us Christians, we're messianic believers. Don't call us a Church, we're a messianic fellowship.*

There is also a reaction from the Gentile believers, who have had issues with the established Church. Many have felt the hurt of the past on behalf of the Jews and seek to make amends, sometimes in dramatic fashion. *We're with you, my Jewish brothers and sisters. We don't want anything to do with the Church that has fostered and promoted anti-Semitism for so long.*

This is reaction, reaction, reaction. What does this give us? It can give us fellowships that are so thoroughly messianic and Hebraic that you'd think you're entering a synagogue with added Jesus. This can't be the true "One New Man", as envisaged by Paul. Yes, you have Jews and Gentiles worshipping Jesus together, but it's not in a balanced way, the scales are rigged, it is over-compensation and does not speak to me as unity in the Body of Christ. Jews and Gentile may be there in body, but in mind and spirit they are drowning in sentimental chicken soup.

Everything within me that speaks of justice, to say nothing of the Jew within, proclaims, *hey you Gentiles have had your chance, surely the times of the Gentiles are now over, it's the turn of the Jews.* Are we saying that we are promoting a form of *reverse* replacement theology? That everything is Jewish now? That all things Gentile must be expunged from the Church (as was the Jewish element all those years ago) and replaced with the Jewish roots? That the Jewish roots should rise from the ground and strangle the whole tree? This can't be right, can it?

So, what am I saying? What is the solution? Well, we can start by removing obstacles to Jewish people from receiving the Gospel of Jesus Christ.

"Again I ask: Did they stumble so as to fall beyond recovery? Not at all! Rather, because of their transgression, salvation has come to the Gentiles to make Israel envious."
(Romans 11:11)

Paul lays it down quite clearly. The Jews as a whole have stumbled and missed out, but God hasn't given up on them but expects them to look at Gentile Christians with envy and say, *"I want what they've got."*

I want what they've got. Can they honestly look at today's Church and say that? The Church has treated Jews horrendously in the past, but that is all behind us now and we must look to the present and the future. We need to look again at "One New Man".

> *"Therefore, remember that formerly you who are Gentiles by birth and called 'uncircumcised' by those who call themselves 'the circumcision' (that done in the body by the hands of men) – remember that at that time you were separate from Christ, excluded from citizenship in Israel and foreigners to the covenants of the promise, without hope and without God in the world. But now in Christ Jesus you who once were far away have been brought near through the blood of Christ. For he himself is our peace, who has made the two one and has destroyed the barrier, the dividing wall of hostility, by abolishing in his flesh the law with its commandments and regulations. **His purpose was to create in himself one new man out of the two**, thus making peace, and in this one body to reconcile both of them to God through the cross, by which he put to death their hostility."*
> (Ephesians 2:11–16, emphasis added)

Historically this never happened. If it had then this book would probably be unnecessary, because the Greek elements would never have made such inroads into our biblical faith. The Jewish elements would have flourished and formed solid foundations for the House of God that would have been built up and dwelt in by Jews and Gentiles, in equal partnership.

Of course this is all conjecture and fanciful thinking and we can only deal with what has been handed down to us. The past is done with but the worst thing we can do is to allow it to shackle us, to hold us back, believing that it's too late to change our ways. It is NEVER too late to change our ways. God Himself is going to do something new with the Jews one day:

> *"Israel has experienced a hardening in part until the full number of the Gentiles has come in. And so all Israel will be saved . . . "*
> (Romans 11:25–26, part)

God hasn't given up on the Jewish people and neither should we. We have to believe that "One New Man" is indeed going to happen in its fullest sense and we can do our bit to clear the way. There is a Jewish tradition at Passover time called *Bedikat chametz*. It is a search and destroy mission for any leavened bread in the house before the festival is celebrated. The house is scoured from top to bottom with the precision of a military campaign and any bread found is burned. As this leavened bread symbolises the sin in our lives, the intent is clearly to attain some degree of purity.

We too must do the same for the Church. We must search and destroy anything unbiblical that is obstructing our walk with the Lord, particularly that which is born out of pagan minds, starting with Plato.

"Therefore, since we are surrounded by such a great cloud of witnesses, let us throw off everything that hinders and the sin that so easily entangles, and let us run with perseverance the race marked out for us."
(Hebrews 12:1)

It is time to get right with God and what better way to start than to *throw off everything that hinders*. It's not going to happen overnight but remember what the ancient Chinese philosopher said, "the longest journey begins with a single step". We have to start somewhere and later on I will provide some pointers.

The "One New Man" movement has always concentrated on the restoration of the Hebrew Roots of Christianity, the Jewish element. As you have seen, the Hebraic approach speaks of God and ways of getting nearer to Him and understanding His ways. The Hebrew Roots represent an expression of faith. But it also represents how we express and exercise this faith. Let's take an example and who better to provide us with an example than Jesus Himself, in fact a twelve-year-old Jesus.

"Every year his parents went to Jerusalem for the Feast of the Passover. When he was twelve years old, they went up to the Feast, according to the custom. After the Feast was over, while his parents were returning home, the boy Jesus stayed behind in Jerusalem, but they were unaware of it. Thinking he was in their company, they travelled on for a day. Then they began looking for him among their relatives and friends. When they did not find him, they went back to Jerusalem to look for him. After three days they found him in the temple courts, sitting among the teachers, listening to them and asking them questions. Everyone who heard him was amazed at his understanding and his answers."

(Luke 2:41–47)

Here we see Jesus asking questions and amazing the teachers with His understanding. There were a lot of questions being asked, by both parties. This is not surprising as the use of questions is a thoroughly Hebraic teaching method. Questions have always been a feature of the Jewish experience. It's often been said that Jews often answer a question by posing a new one. *Are you sure about that?* Why do you ask? *How do you feel?* How should I feel?

Somewhere in suburbia a group of friends are meeting in the front room of a house. They are Christians and this is a Thursday night house group meeting and there is a special guest. It is a Messianic Rabbi (a teacher who believes in Jesus) and he is going to demonstrate this teaching method.

Rabbi (to Bob) : Who killed Jesus?

There's an awkward silence as Bob tries to think of an answer that shows insight, maturity and political correctness. The Rabbi senses this and pre-empts him.

Rabbi: Bob, the first thing that entered your mind, that's what I want. Now . . . who killed Jesus?

Bob: The Romans.

Rabbi: What, all Romans? Be specific please?

Bob: The soldiers. The Roman soldiers who executed him.

Rabbi: Ah, the soldiers. Tell me, do soldiers always act on their initiative? Was it their idea or . . . ?

Bob: No, of course not. They were following orders.

Rabbi: Whose orders, Bob?

Bob: Well, of their superiors. Then you're going to ask, "who instructed *them*", aren't you, Rabbi. I suppose the buck stopped with Pontius Pilate, then. He gave the initial orders.

Rabbi: Yes Bob, good thinking. But I *do* have to go a bit deeper here. After all, Pontius Pilate must have had good cause to give this command. So . . . who gave him this good cause? Who killed Jesus?

Bob: Well the Bible talks of the Jewish mob who were baying for Jesus' blood . . .

Rabbi: So the Jews killed Jesus?

Bob: Um . . .

Rabbi: OK. Awkward moment here. Let's delve deeper, Bob. Who were the actual people crying, "Crucify Him"?

Bob: That would be the Jewish mob outside Pilate's palace.

Rabbi: And, in your experience, do mobs act on their own initiative, or are they usually led by others?

Bob: Well yes. Someone must have stirred them up, I suppose.

Rabbi: So there would be some Jewish agitators, who would have influenced the mob?

Bob: That seems to make sense.

Rabbi: And could you venture a guess as to the identity of these agitators?

Bob: Um . . .

Rabbi: Who had been Jesus' main opponents in those days?

Bob: The religious leaders? Scribes and Pharisees?

Rabbi: So it was the religious establishment that riled the mob? So it was these Jewish leaders who killed Jesus then?

Bob: Yes . . . I suppose so.

Rabbi: Are you sure? Let me rephrase the question, then. Who actually was responsible for the death of Jesus?

Bob: Isn't that the same question?

Rabbi: Then let me expand on this. What does it say in Matthew 16:21?

After a pause.

Bob: From that time on Jesus began to explain to his disciples that he must go to Jerusalem and suffer many things at the hands of the elders, chief priests and teachers of the law, and that he must be killed and on the third day be raised to life.

Rabbi: What does this tell you?

Bob: That Jesus knew in advance . . .

Rabbi: Correct. And . . .

Bob: I suppose if he knew it was going to happen, then it was all in God's plan. But, it still needed the Jews and the Romans to actually do it. Surely they had free will in the matter?

Rabbi: Correct again. You're getting the hang of this, Bob. But there's one thing more. Do you remember what Jesus said on the cross?

Bob: It is finished?

Rabbi: No, earlier than that. What did he say about those who had put him on that cross?

Bob: Oh yes, I know. *Father forgive them, for they know not what they do.*

Rabbi: Correct. So where did the responsibility lie with the death of Jesus?

Bob: Well the Jews pushed for it and the Romans did the deed but . . .

Rabbi: Yes?

Bob: They didn't know why they were doing it and Jesus forgave them.

Rabbi: That's right. So who was responsible?

Bob: Jesus Himself?

Rabbi: It seems so, but there are some words in John, chapter 10, verses 17 to 18 . . . Can you find this?

After a pause.

Bob: *"The reason my Father loves me is that I lay down my life – only to take it up again. No one takes it from me, but I lay it down of* *my own accord. I have authority to lay it down and authority to take it up again. This command I received from my Father."*

Rabbi: Who is speaking here?

Bob: Jesus.

Rabbi: And who asked Him to lay down His life?

Bob: God.

Rabbi: So who was responsible for the death of Jesus?

Bob: God.

There's silence for a few moments.

Sue: For God so loved the world that He gave His one and only Son . . .

Jim: . . . that whoever believes in Him . . .

Bob: Wow. These words now seem so alive . . .

If you retrace the conversation you will notice that all the Rabbi did was ask questions and allowed Bob to reach the conclusions by himself, until a clear understanding was reached.

Isn't that wonderful, *a clear understanding*. How many of us, if we are really honest with ourselves, have a clear understanding of the things of God? Apart from the *mysteries*, of course, that we will never have an inkling of this side of heaven!

The sermon is a great tool for imparting and receiving wisdom and for many folk – Sunday Christians we call them – it's the only way. But what about those *reluctant* Sunday Christians, especially men, who resent being asked to dress respectfully, enter a strange building, be nice to everyone, don't swear, smoke or spit and then sit down in silence and listen to someone drone on for up to an hour without interruption. Is this how things are done in the *real world* in the twenty-first century? Is this how we get our daily news, or our workplace instructions? Even school classrooms are temples of interactivity these days. But Christians or seekers are dragged along to hear a lecture.

Of course it works for some, don't knock it. But the sermon in its current form (apart from the Powerpoint stuff) was invented by seventeenth-century Puritans and a population brought up on the 30 second advert and the Simpsons do not have the attention span of a seventeenth-century Puritan! And I'm not embarrassed to admit that I include myself in that number! If you think about it, the sermon is quite a Platonic concept, as a one-way flow of knowledge from the "spiritual" preacher to the congregation.

Nevertheless many have been brought into the Kingdom through the efforts of a good preacher, so I am not knocking it, just offering new possibilities. A Hebraic way of doing things would be a small gathering where everyone shared according to their gifts. Of course some would have preaching or teaching gifts, but how more satisfying it would be if these gifts were shared in an interactive environment. I have recently helped launch a ministry, *Saffron Planet*, which simply involves eight ordinary people, miked up, sitting around a table and chatting about ordinary things, from a Christian perspective. Our goal is to thrash things out in order to get a *clear understanding* of the things of God. It's not grand or fancy and anybody can do it, but it has been very effective as a podcast, winning two awards within six months of launch (not that I'm boasting of course). The point is that, although the sermon is still valid as a Christian communication tool, it doesn't have to be the only way.

Let's take our lead from the very first Christians.

> *"They devoted themselves to the apostles' teaching and to the fellowship, to the breaking of bread and to prayer."*
> (Acts 2:42)

The apostles' teaching? Well they had the apostles there in person, so you can imagine what lively discussions they must have had and what a privilege it would have been for those early Christians to pow-wow with men who had sat at the feet of the Master.

We Christians seem to have lost our reasoning ability, or perhaps it has never been encouraged, so the "reasoning muscle" in our brain has withered and died through lack of use. It almost seems that we have fulfilled the stereotype of the mind-free Christian, people of faith without reason, people without a *clear understanding*.

Let's face it, that's how the world sees us and when they switch on their Satellite TVs and roam through the God slots, there is little there to make them think otherwise. They see mega-church services, pews packed with apparent automatons, swaying to repetitive rock riffs, orchestrated by a showy performer on the platform. This could be a rock concert, albeit with audience participation and donation buckets. They see passionate appeals for cash, rewarded by green prayer clothes, Holy Land oil or the latest leather-bound Bible, adorned with dubious wisdom from your favourite preacher.

They see earnest teachers pouring forth from a particular theological standpoint and do not have the discernment to differentiate between the sheep and the goats. This is what people see when they tune in and however much real quality there may be in places, the uninitiated do not have the tools to know when the truth is being preached.

"For the time will come when men will not put up with sound doctrine. Instead, to suit their own desires, they will gather around them a great number of teachers to say what their itching ears want to hear."

(2 Timothy 4:3)

Are we Christians so full of faith that we have deliberately switched our brains off? Do we really expect to make Jesus attractive to others if we demonstrate such naivete? Where was the witness when many of us filled our sheds with tins and stocked up on water purifiers in 1999, because our pastor, or a TV evangelist or our favourite writer told us that either Y2K was going to herald in a new dark age or Jesus was going to return on New Year's Day to usher in the millennium? Where was the witness when we excitedly boasted of the twenty or so folk raised from the dead in Lakeland, Florida, without any medical corroboration? Where was the witness when yet another "prophet" predicts a specific event that doesn't happen, or publishes their prophecies retrospectively to show their 100% accuracy!

There will always be those who instigate these travesties and God will deal with them in His own good time. But our responsibility lies in our response. How many of us are true Bereans?

> *"Now the Bereans were of more noble character than the Thessalonians, for they received the message with great eagerness and examined the Scriptures every day to see if what Paul said was true."*
> (Acts 17:11)

These folk had the cheek to query even the most anointed, God-centered preacher and teacher of the day, Paul. Oh that we can have such cheek too!

We too need to *examine the Scriptures every day* to see if what the preacher/teacher/TV evangelist says is true, so that we can have a . . . clear understanding.

The Bible encourages us to do so. Here are a few verses

> *"'Come now, let us reason together,'*
>   *says the L*ORD.
> *'Though your sins are like scarlet,*
>   *they shall be as white as snow;*
> *though they are red as crimson,*
>   *they shall be like wool.'"*
> (Isaiah 1:18)

> *"As his custom was, Paul went into the synagogue, and on three Sabbath days he reasoned with them from the Scriptures."*
> (Acts 17:2)

"So he reasoned in the synagogue with the Jews and the God-fearing Greeks, as well as in the marketplace day by day with those who happened to be there."
(Acts 17:17)

"Every Sabbath he reasoned in the synagogue, trying to persuade Jews and Greeks."
(Acts 18:4)

"They arrived at Ephesus, where Paul left Priscilla and Aquila. He himself went into the synagogue and reasoned with the Jews."
(Acts 18:19)

In the Church, faith without reason can produce superstition and strange ideas. Also, reason without faith isn't too clever either and there's a lot of it about in the current Church. It produces compromise, where biblical truths are sacrificed at the altar of Science and "progressive" secularism.

"But in your hearts set apart Christ as Lord. Always be prepared to give an answer to everyone who asks you to give the reason for the hope that you have. But do this with gentleness and respect."
(1 Peter 3:15)

The *reason for the hope,* that just about sums it all up. Are we honestly in a position where we can fulfil this? All it takes is a willingness to explore and be open to where God is leading us.

But where I believe God is taking us next may be uncomfortable for some of you. There's a cost involved. It's not just an acknowledgement of a historical injustice, it's a journey to the very heart of God and His plans for mankind.

It concerns the Jews themselves.

The People of Many Names

14

The Jews are the key to God's heart. When they, as a people, rejected Jesus as their Messiah they broke His heart, but when Christians rejected the Jews, God's heart was broken all over again. Christian anti-Semitism is a blight on history and a stain on the Church and until there is an honest acknowledgement of this fact, the Church is travelling with the handbrake on.

The history of the Jewish people can be condensed into the examination of just two questions:

1. *How have the Jews managed to survive so long?* How many other people have a history that stretches back 4000 years? The Assyrians, still a distinct people after centuries of dispersion, are their only serious competition, though they are over a 1000 years younger.
2. *Why have they been so hated by so many other people for so many different reasons?* Christ-killers, Children of Satan, Child kidnappers, Conspirators of Zion, Capitalists, Communists – and that's just the 'C's!

These questions are connected, though, and should be held in tension with each other. In fact, they can become one question, one urgent, anguished plea:

How have the Jews managed to survive so long *despite* being hated by so many people?

This can be seen to be one of the most central mysteries of history, alongside the big ones (how did life begin?) and knocking the smaller ones (who shot JFK?) into a cocked hat. It's such a big question because it uncovers a drama that has been unfolding for thousands of years, but hidden to most. The drama is a classic conflict between good and evil, between two great powers that have been in opposition since time began. If we concede this possibility, then perhaps the evidence can start to make sense. We can see that the reason that the Jews have survived so long is that a Great Power has been *protecting* them and that the reason why they have been hated for so long is that another great power has been *attacking* them. This provides us with an answer to our key question.

The reason the Jews have managed to survive so long despite being hated by so many people is because the power that is protecting them is *greater* than the power that has been attacking them. God against Satan, the devil. No contest.

The story is told of King Louis XIV of France asking Blaise Pascal for a proof of the existence of God. The reply was immediate. *"The Jews, your majesty"*, replied Pascal.

Why on earth should this be? Could the evidence we have presented be so smothered by the fingerprints of God, that a forensic sceptic would have to be blinkered to ignore it? Can the story of the Jews really point us to God? Can you think of any other explanations? It is, in my estimation, one of the most powerful apologetics for the existence of God and not to be dismissed lightly.

We can imagine King Louis asking a second question, asking Pascal for a proof of the existence of the devil. Equally immediately the answer could have come. *"Anti-Semitism, your majesty"*, would be the reply, *"hatred of the Jews."*

The question that we asked – how have the Jews managed

to survive so long *despite* being hated by so many people? – cannot be answered by referring to the wisdom of historians, philosophers, psychologists, politicians or sociologists. They have all failed. There is only one solution, a *spiritual* one, but, in our materialist way of peering at the world, it's probably the last thing we want to hear. It goes against the grain of our secular world-system, but that doesn't make it any less true.

The truth is so plain to see that we should be shouting it from the treetops. There is an awesome unseen battle going on for our hearts and minds. It's a battle that will continue long after we die and, indeed, the consequences of this battle affect all of us regardless of whether we believe in God or the devil or whatever. At the end of your life you will be pitched into this battle whether you like it or not, whether you have lived your life as a committed Christian or a committed atheist. Truth is truth, it's not all in the eye of the beholder, it's a solid, unchanging truth that is going to determine where you end up after death.

To help your understanding on why a loving God could allow the Holocaust, it may help to look at the situation from a different angle. God could have chosen to protect His "chosen people" through these turbulent times when anti-Semitism has ruled the roost. To counter the seeds of hatred planted in the heart of men against the Jews by the devil, God could instead have put a supernatural love in the heart of all Christians, but surely that would have taken away their free will (the devil has no problem with people's free will, he just wishes to dominate and influence souls in the best way he can). In the final analysis we all have free will to make our own decisions, whether to accept Jesus as our Saviour or whether to love or hate God's "chosen people", the Jews. The choice is yours – it's free, but there is, ultimately a cost, so use it wisely.

I will now bow to the insights and knowledge of the late lamented Derek Prince to furnish an explanation as to why Christians have historically treated Jews so badly. In his teaching letter (No. 7) on *The Root of Anti-Semitism*, he says this:

"While I was preaching in our local church in Jerusalem, quite unexpect-edly I heard myself say, 'Anti-Semitism can be summed up in one word – MESSIAH!!' At that moment I understood that from its beginning Anti-Semitism had one source – Satan – who was motivated by the knowledge that the One who was to be his conqueror, the Messiah, would come through a people that would be specially prepared by God."

He goes on to explain that the Jews, the people in question, were targets of Satan through their whole history, either through being enticed into idolatry (early history) or through complete destruction (later history). The reason for this hatred is that he knows that his days are numbered, a countdown culminating in the return of Jesus the Messiah. But this event won't happen until two conditions are fulfilled.

Firstly, the Christian gospel is to be preached to all nations, *"And this gospel of the kingdom will be preached in all the world as a witness to all the nations, and then the end will come"* (Matthew 24:14).

Secondly, the Jews must be in place and in a position to ask Jesus to return. In Matthew 23:38–39, Jesus had said to the Jews in Jerusalem, *"See, your house is left to you desolate, for I say to you, you shall see Me no more till you say, 'Blessed is He who comes in the name of the Lord.'"*

The Jews must be in place, in this final drama at the end of all things, to ask Jesus to return. Who knows what the circum-stances will be, but they are likely to be fairly extreme and desperate. Their hearts will be ready, the hardening spoken of in the last chapter would have been broken down. As it says in Zechariah 12:10: *"And I will pour on the house of David and on the inhabitants of Jerusalem the Spirit of grace and supplication; then they will look on Me whom they have pierced; they will mourn for Him as one mourns for his only son, and grieve for Him as one grieves for a first-born."*

And when they do that . . . anti-Semitism would be no more, because the root cause of it would have been taken away. I pray that those Christians who have been hardened to Israel and the Jewish people don't have to wait until then to realise the truth of their errors.

> "'Shout and be glad, O Daughter of Zion. For I am coming, and I will live among you,' declares the LORD. 'Many nations will be joined with the LORD in that day and will become my people. I will live among you and you will know that the LORD Almighty has sent me to you. The LORD will inherit Judah as his portion in the holy land and will again choose Jerusalem.'"
> (Zechariah 2:10–12)

At that time God's scales of justice will take a sudden swing in favour of His people, the Jews. When that happens, all who have perpetrated anti-Semitism, who have acted against "the apple of His eye", will be punished accordingly. By that time the Jews, who have been scattered to the four winds, would have returned to their land, Israel. In this future time God will live with His people, who will be taken from all nations.

So how is all this relevant? Let's reconsider our "One New Man".

> "Therefore, remember that formerly you who are Gentiles by birth and called 'uncircumcised' by those who call themselves 'the circumcision' (that done in the body by the hands of men) – remember that at that time you were separate from Christ, excluded from citizenship in Israel and foreigners to the covenants of the promise, without hope and without God in the world. But now in Christ Jesus you who once were far away have been brought near through the blood of Christ. For he himself is our peace, who has made the two one and has destroyed the barrier, the dividing wall of hostility, by abolishing in his flesh the law with its commandments and regulations. **His purpose was to create in himself one new man out of the two**, thus making peace, and in this one body to reconcile both of them to God through the cross, by which he put to death their hostility."
> (Ephesians 2:11–16, emphasis added)

One New Man, eh? We Jews may be able to forgive, but it's awfully hard to forget. Certain events and people are fixed in the memory. John Chrysostom (a Church Father who preached hatred against the Jews), The Crusades, The Inquisition, Martin Luther (turned against the Jews later in life, after failing to convert them!), pogroms, expulsions, the Holocaust. Although there is no space here for detailed explanations, all of these were birthed within a Christian context. We need to negotiate a peace treaty to end all others, between two parties who have been at war for nearly 2,000 years. And it has hardly been an even conflict, with all the casualties on one side. Only the Holy Spirit could broker such a deal, but this deal requires certain conditions to be met by both parties.

The Jewish Christian must search deep within and set aside historical injustices, even if they have impacted on him personally, and not harbour any resentment or misplaced feelings of superiority. He must recognise that there are jewels among the dross, there have been good people, noble acts and worthy teachings that have had the mark of true Christianity. Many sacrifices have been made by faithful Christians to ensure that the true Word of God has been preached and that the faith has survived the centuries intact. Not all Christians have wanted to kill Jews. The Jewish believer must not be provoked or tempted into over-reaction, as I mentioned earlier, by overloading this new partnership, as a way of over-compensating for centuries of imbalance. The Jew has a lot to offer, but there is such a thing as *too much of a good thing* and he must always seek for balance.

The Gentile Christian must also search deep within, for any trace of anti-Semitism because this is no political or military peace, where resentments still fester and the peace is just a stop-gap until the next war. There has to be a true and open desire to welcome their Jewish brother and sister as partners in the Body of Christ. This has to be an everlasting and unconditional peace, undergirded by a pure heart.

It's all very well you Gentiles drinking from the rich pool of Hebraic thought, culture and learning and neglecting the very people who made it all happen. This is key to the whole enterprise and the next chapter will give suggestions on how we can get the whole thing to work.

CHAPTER 15

Finding One New Home

So far this book has meandered all over the place, though hopefully not so randomly as to lose the plot. It was never my intention to pile on the facts and leave you high and dry and not sure where to go next, if indeed you felt the need to actually do something next. Hopefully I have provoked you into some form of action, so the task now is to decide what practical actions can flow from all the new knowledge that is rattling around inside your brain.

But first, in developing the theme introduced in the previous chapter, we must again think of the Jewish people. Whatever you take on board, in terms of actions, one thing must be stressed. *One New Man* is a partnership between people – Jews and Gentiles – not just ideas. It is not good enough just to take Jewish ideas and run with them, in the knowledge that the vast proportion of Jewish people are currently spiritually lost and that a contributory factor to this situation has been the actions of Christians, past and present.

In the past, Jews were persecuted by Christians *in the name of Christ*, so it is not surprising that Jews currently are not exactly embracing the religion of Jesus Christ. In the present, many Christians, acting out of misplaced compassion for the past, are in fact totally deluded in their attitude to the Jews. They shy away from evangelising them because of the past hurts and, *aren't they still God's people and saved through Judaism?* This is totally wrong and just a subtle form of anti-Semitism, denying Jews eternal life at the altar of political correctness. Every unsaved Jew is going to hell just the same as any unsaved Gentile.

> *"There is neither Jew nor Greek, slave nor free, male nor female, for you are all one in Christ Jesus."*
> (Galatians 3:28)

Our first thought should be to look at our *One New Man* and realise how lopsided he is. Not enough Jews! So how do we get more Jews in? Simple – we make a concerted effort to pray for them, love them, understand them and make sensitive efforts, if led, to present the Gospel to them. We must learn to treat them at least as any other people group and realise their need for the Good News of Jesus Christ. Forget political correctness and inter-faith wishy-washyness, we need to do our bit to get them into the Kingdom.

Now the scene has been set, let's consider some practical actions. Of course you may not be in a position to do everything I suggest, but everything you do will bless you, because God said it would. Here He speaks of Abraham and his descendants.

> *"I will bless those who bless you, and whoever curses you I will curse . . . "*
> (Genesis 12:3)

Blessings are not to be sniffed at and it's a win-win situation. You bless the Jews, God blesses you. It won't necessarily make you rich, healthy or beautiful, but if it leads just one of God's *chosen people* to salvation, then you have blessed that person immeasurably, which in turn blesses you too!

We start with something that every Christian can do, what every Christian ought to be doing . . . praying. Pray for the Jewish people and, if there's one particular focus to your prayers, be inspired by the following.

> *"I do not want you to be ignorant of this mystery, brothers, so that you may not be conceited: Israel has experienced a hardening in part until the full number of the Gentiles has come in."*
> (Romans 11:25)

There is a mystery here, something known only to God. Paul has revealed this to the Gentiles as an explanation as to why Jews, by and large, reject the Gospel of Jesus Christ. *It's all about you, Gentiles, all about you!* God, for His own reasons, has hardened most of the Jewish people against the Gospel and, through this hardening, has switched His attention to Gentiles. It's a mystery, so His reasons for this may not be clear to us, but it does help us to get things into perspective. This is why our One New Man is lopsided. But there's a time limit on this and, one day, this hardening is going to be removed and, what a day that is going to be! Read on . . .

> *"Rather, because of their transgression, salvation has come to the Gentiles to make Israel envious. But if their transgression means riches for the world, and their loss means riches for the Gentiles, how much greater riches will their fullness bring!"*
> (Romans 11:11–12)

One day our One New Man is going to be complete and the world is going to be blessed because of the greater riches this will bring. I believe we are close, very close to this day. We are not there yet but, inasmuch as God answers the sincere prayers of His people, we can pray that this day can come soon. This should be the primary focus of your prayers for the Jewish people.

> *"Even to this day when Moses is read, a veil covers their hearts."*
> (2 Corinthians 3:15)

Pray for this veil to be lifted, so the Jews can truly see Jesus and claim their spiritual inheritance. Of course you may know individual Jews, or God may have burdened you to pray for Israel.

> "*Pray for the peace of Jerusalem:*
>   '*May those who love you be secure.*'"
> (Psalm 122:6)

Whatever God leads you to do, just do it!

Next, let's think about your home life. To the religious Jew, as we have seen, the home is the focal point of everything, not just a place to sleep, eat and watch TV. Of course, the Jewish home environment is a development over centuries, combining a unique history of isolationism with strict religious guidelines. This is not something that can be artificially emulated and I am not asking you to, yet there is a lot that we can learn just from one aspect, which is the central role of the family unit.

Of course these days the family unit takes on many guises, with many households not even being fully blood-related (step-families, friends sharing a house etc.), but we have to start somewhere. Here are some suggestions, though of course it implies that the whole household is amenable to changes and we are not going to have a situation of *come on you lot, I have spoken, just get in line or else!* On the other hand, you may have your home life sussed. A stable, God-fearing family home is not a Jewish patent. Many Christian families have bucked the trend and have created a godly home environment. If this is you, then be commended, but still read on, because there still may be more that you can learn to make it even better.

Start thinking about God's presence in every room of your house. Acknowledge Him as being interested in all areas of your life, however mundane and un-spiritual it may seem. Make it a habit of praying after meals. You've already eaten, feeling relaxed and satisfied. Now's a good time to thank God for this blessing. After the prayer, stay seated and use this time to discuss stuff. It doesn't have to be a Bible study or devotional, God is interested in all aspects of your life, so, whatever you discuss, include Him in the conversation!

Don't let the prayers become dry rituals. Never forget that God has a sense of humour (He created *you*, after all!) and it would be fun to include special thank-yous for specific foodstuffs. *Bless You for the broccoli, something that tastes so bad must be doing me some good!* Get to the realisation that prayer is just conversation with an unseen guest and just learn to keep in tension the fact that this particular unseen guest was also responsible for creating the Universe and all that is within it.

These days a typical home has so many distractions, but by far the worst are those that tie up an individual into their own little world, to the exclusion of everyone else. The worst example of this is the computer game and this is something I should know about, as a computer game designer back in the 1980s, when it all started. My game designs were all worthy and family-orientated, which is why I nearly went bankrupt, failing to realise that all folk really wanted to do was to kill aliens and rescue fair maidens. Since then we managed to get all three of our boys through their teenage years without the whiff of a Nintendo or Sony games console, encouraging them to develop their creative gifts and social skills. Before I sink into sepia-toned nostalgia, my point is that we must learn to appreciate and engage with those who share our home, even though society tells us never to cross the generation gap. Jewish families historically have housed four generations in one home and I know of one Gentile family that does this to great effect – grandmother, parents, children (and one husband) and granddaughter all living together in harmony, helping each other and communicating together, with God as the centre of the household. Remember one thing – the teenager didn't exist before the 1950s, teenagers were invented by the marketing men to make money out of rock and roll!

Education is important. Remember, to the religious Jewish mind, study is the highest form of worship. Here is a practical suggestion. You will have heard of home groups, indeed many churches include them in their weekly programme, but have you heard of a *Beit Midrash*? Literally a "house of study", every synagogue includes one within its premises as a place for earnest discussion of God's Word. Currently there is a growing movement of creating a *Beit Midrash* in a home environment. Think of a typical home group, with a leader, study notes and fixed programme, then think again, but start with a clean slate.

All very well, you may ask, *but how does one get started?* Well, for a start, it doesn't require a leader in the traditional sense. The Greek model would have the pastor, minister, elder or teacher leading the meeting, as in a traditional church service or home group and using the meeting as a different way of teaching. A *Beit Midrash* doesn't need to be led with someone who has prepared well, or has all the answers. It needs a facilitator, someone to move things along, but the whole point of it is for everyone to learn together. If your minister wants to join in, then he's on the same level as everyone else and should not be allowed to dominate. The point of the Beit Midrash is the acknowledgement that sometimes we don't have all the answers, but it will be fun to find them out together. Proceedings are disorderly, a very Jewish idea, with interruptions, silences, jokes and tangential thinking all the norm. The one thing you won't need to do is put your hand up to speak, though you may have to deal sensitively with the situation of everyone speaking at once. The best way to try this form of group study is just suck it and see . . . so what's holding you back, just try it!

Another thing you may want to consider at home is to hold a Passover service. It's the most accessible of Jewish festivals for Christians, but it will need to be done sensitively and relevantly. Sensitivity is needed because this is the most Jewish of all festivals, commemorating the greatest Hebrew prophet of all, Moses, and the greatest event in Jewish biblical history, the Exodus from Egypt. Even secular Jewish homes have been known to occasionally do a Passover Seder night, which is not surprising as it is the most evocative of all, a feast for all five senses and food . . . lots of it.

If you decide to start to celebrate Passover in your home it is best to use one of the messianic *haggadahs* (orders of service) that are available, that use Passover in a Christian context, as an understanding of the circumstances and setting of Jesus' Last Supper (I can recommend the *Christ in Passover* DVD by Chris Hill, available at clministries.org.uk). It will also help you gain an understanding of the Jewish context of the Exodus, which must not be forgotten. The worst thing you can do is strip out the Jewish elements, but the best thing you can do is invite any Jewish friends you have and, whether they have much of an understanding or not, use them as advisors on the project. Show them that you are not hijacking their festival, but just want to get a better understanding of the Jewish roots of your faith. Whether or not there are any Jewish people at the Passover service you must always make an effort to pray for the Jewish people as part of the liturgy. It's the least you can do.

Of course the Passover service can be a grander affair. This takes us out of our homes and into the traditional church environment. Many churches hold Passover services, using a set liturgy (usually the messianic haggadahs mentioned earlier). Again, the same rules apply, but more so, as this is likely to come to the attention of the local Jewish community. Be sensitive, perhaps even send an invitation to the local synagogue, though, if you do so, inform them first why you are celebrating Passover and what form the service is taking.

Other Jewish festivals can also be considered, though the lesser festivals of Purim and Chanukah are not to be encouraged, as these are more nationalistic and jingoistic, with the personal theme of triumph over anti-Semitism, by the Persians and Greeks respectively. *Shavuot* is a neglected festival and any liturgy that combines the twin themes of the Word and Spirit is to be encouraged. *Sukkot* is perhaps the most relevant festival for churches to consider, with a secondary theme of Jews and

Gentiles celebrating the future millennial rule of Jesus. This is why Israel tourism from Christians peaks at this time of the year. Every Sukkot, a colourful procession through Jerusalem is staged by Christians from all over the world, with tour groups virtually falling over each other in a very congested Holy Land.

Again, if you choose to celebrate any of these festivals in your church, or in the local community, be proactive in involving the Jewish community and make provisions within the service for prayer for the salvation of the Jew. Don't worry about offending them, be bold and go for it – you know what's best for them, their eternal salvation is at issue here. They may huff and puff, or show general indifference, but, as long as it is sensitively done, let love and sincerity be your motivations, rather than just lip service and they will respect you for it.

Apart from the festivals, it will be hard to suddenly introduce Jewish elements to traditional church services. Prayer is the easiest thing to get started, perhaps arranging a "Prayer for Israel" group to meet regularly. It would be foolish to start urging the minister to dump the sermon, liturgy and prayer/ hymn sandwich because they are suddenly "too Greek". Introducing Jewish elements is more relevant in a smaller scale, as already mentioned, so perhaps experimenting with the *Beit Midrash* idea for home groups would be a good place to start.

Finally, my big idea. Perhaps it is time we started to look at the Hebraic way of worshipping God. Perhaps we haven't thought big enough when we think of our BIG God. Knowing that He values every part of us, body, mind and spirit, perhaps we should be worshipping Him, *body, mind and spirit*. It's time to think new, to think big. This has been a *big* paragraph, it's time to explain. Just imagine the following . . .

Posters adorn shop fronts, leaflets thrust into unsuspecting hands. A new Christian worship centre is opening up in town. Groans give way to piqued interest as the text of the leaflets doesn't follow the usual script.

Come along to NewTown Church and worship God in new ways. Something for everyone and everything for the glory of God. Music, dance, arts & crafts, drama, discussions, writing and poetry classes, Hebrew lessons. Open all hours.

Is worship all about nice songs, ancient and modern? Worship is about all we can give back to God. Worship is about dance, particularly within the framework of modest dress and behaviour. Worship is about study of God's Word, either individually or in discussion and argument. Worship is about the creative arts, writing and performing drama, poetry, prose, pottery or papier mâché. Worship is the exercise of all the gifts and talents that God has given you, given back to Him, to bless Him and others. Do we really need specialists to lead us into God's presence? Surely there must be room for a model that involves ALL of God's people, exercising their gifts and talents in a nurturing communal atmosphere, blessing each other and blessing God in the process. Isn't this worship, too? It's worth thinking about, isn't it?

These days most Christian initiatives for worship, prayer and celebrating our faith are big corporate events, the bigger the better. Through radio, TV and the Web, the whole world can watch major events, beamed out from packed stadiums and conference centres, but are now multiplied in coverage through cable, wireless and the airwaves. Global Day of Prayer, The Call, world conferences, crusades and rallies for teens, women, men, Pentecostals and whatever. Big, big, BIG! Everything has to be global, world-reaching, mega-this and mega-that and I ask the simple question, Why?

The world creates ever taller buildings, ever faster cars, ever more powerful computers. It's the Tower of Babel revisited! Every year a whole swathe of world records is broken by athletes, sometimes even without drugs. Does the twenty-first century Christian Church need to take on these strivings and ideals? Does it need to have maximum coverage for everything it does? Do we need to be saying *our religion is bigger than yours, taller than yours?*

We have the truth, we know that. Sometimes we need to shout it from the hilltops, sometimes the Great Commission impels us to think big and act bigger. But is this the best way? Just because the World does it, should the Church? Just because we now have broadcast delivery systems that can beam sound and pictures into your TV from anywhere in the world, does it mean that we have to broadcast everything that is happening in our Christian subculture? Is this God's way, is this how Jesus did it? If Jesus had a Sony PD150 TV camera and a portable TV broadcast system would the feeding of the 5,000 have cured world famine? Would the Sermon on the Mount have brought about world peace? Can the "anointing" be digitised and transmitted electronically? Can we truly be healed by touching our TV sets?

Or does God work best as that still, small voice, away from the noise and the clamour, in the privacy of your own space, with fellow Christian sojourners, in your home or in small groups. This is the Hebraic way and I believe this is still the best way for the Church to move forwards. It may take longer, but then look at revivals from the past to see how swiftly and effectively whole nations were turned round just by a small group of people powerfully used by God, using just the power of individual voices, carried from place to place by foot or horseback.

But here's a warning, addressed to those who have already "walked on the Hebraic side". There are many folk, both Jews and Gentiles, who have already taken on these new expressions wholeheartedly. In many cases it has been just a "dip in the water", perhaps an occasional Passover service in the church hall, or Hebrew lessons at the local synagogue. But others have gone further.

Messianic fellowships have been founded, where Jews and Gentiles meet together, with an emphasis given to a Hebraic expression of faith in the teaching, liturgy and worship. They tend to still be predominantly Gentile in the UK, with typically no more than 30% of the membership being from a Jewish background. In areas with few Jews I have heard of some such fellowships with not a single Jew in the congregation. One can respect and understand the needs and motivation behind such expressions of faith, but one can also sense the dangers.

Imagine an unsaved Jew arriving at a messianic fellowship with few (or no) Jews, where Hebrew songs are sung, Jewish festivals are celebrated and where many of the prayers are based on the Jewish prayer book. Would this be a good witness to a Jew, conscious of a history of persecution and hatred by the Christian world? His immediate impression is to see the natural and horrific conclusion of seventeen centuries of Jewish persecution at the hands of Christians. *They have stolen our possessions, our wellbeing, and our lives and now they steal our culture and heritage! Have they left us nothing?*

I have been to such fellowships where Gentiles have worn skullcaps and prayer shawls, speak Yiddish and declare, in their testimony, that Messianic Judaism (rather than Jesus) has saved them! I know this is an extreme case, but Gentiles, particularly those who profess to love the Jewish people, must realise that *salvation has come to the Gentiles to make Israel envious* (Romans 11:11), *to make them long for what has been lost.* It is not to make Israel *angry!* Are your actions in accordance with this biblical command?

Gentile Christians who have studied the Jewish roots of their faith have been mightily enriched, particularly when they are able to teach others in their churches or worship with like-minded believers in messianic fellowships. But – and this is a BIG BUT – unless there is a genuine and demonstrable love for the Jewish people – it is a selfish exercise, carried out just for personal blessing. It may bless you but in no way is it blessing the Jewish people or providing a balance in our expressions of our faith. Sure, you can learn from the Jewish roots, but don't neglect the very people who literally shed their blood to ensure that these teachings have survived to enrich you. It's not rocket science. Just treat your Jewish neighbour first as a human being and the Holy Spirit will do the rest.

But there's another danger with these fellowships, particularly when they are named Messianic *synagogues* and are predominantly Jewish in membership. Two extremes are to be avoided.

Firstly, at all times it must always be the Bible that is the foundational reference, not the Talmud, Midrash, the Joy of Yiddish, or the Jewish Chronicle. Hopefully you get my drift here. The primary emphasis must be biblical teaching, in a Hebraic environment, not Hebraic culture first. Using technical terms, these fellowships must be *Christocentric* (centred on Christ) and not *ethnocentric* (centred on Jewish culture). We must always remember that it is Jesus who is worshipped, even if he is Yeshua and wears a yarmulke (skullcap). Torah is not to be worshipped, nor the Sabbath, however it is dressed up. Jewish festivals are a blessing and fantastic teaching tools, as you've already seen, but they are not compulsory and not a salvation issue.

Secondly, don't forget that *One New Man* is Jew and Gentile working in partnership, each with his own distinctive. Jew is Jew and Gentile is Gentile. To be Gentile is not to be a wannabee Jew, so don't accept any teaching that seems to imply that you've somehow got to become more Jewish! Also never accept any teaching, dear Gentile, that implies that you're a second class citizen in the Kingdom of Heaven. All that I can say about that is that it is some kind of sick joke in a clumsy attempt to reverse the role of the medieval Jew in the Christian world, when we were forced to wear a yellow star, considered to be vermin and not allowed to look a good "Christian" in the eye! Some messianic fellowships have a two-tier membership structure, with Jew and Gentile treated differently and a Gentile never allowed into full membership. If heaven is not going to be like that, then neither should churches or fellowships. 'Nuff said!

Epilogue

Of course a whole universe of new thoughts and ideas have been crammed into this little book. This is just a primer and I have just created sketches of the subjects covered. But, to paraphrase the apostle John, if I covered everything that needed to be said, surely the whole world would not have room for all the books that could be written. Literary license mixed with Jewish exaggeration, in my case, but there's an awful lot more that could be covered. Nevertheless, one has to start somewhere and perhaps I will be freed up to write a few more sequels to expand on these ideas.

A prominent Christian magazine recently featured an article entitled "Walking ancient paths". It was one of the most popular features they've had, I was reliably informed. It highlighted the current unrest in some Christians with the way things are, with a hankering back, nostalgically, to the way things were, *because surely things were better then?* Yet the article didn't quite do what it said on the tin. It didn't go the full way, but stopped off before the end of the journey. Ancient traditions were described, but these were the traditions of the Catholic and Orthodox Churches. It was bells, smells, icons, quietness and incense. What a shame they didn't look back further to the days when the Church was thoroughly biblical, before the corruption of Greek influence. In a way it was not the fault of the article writer, because little is really known about those far-off times and it's hard to be nostalgic about something lost in the bowels of history. But, perhaps, this book may help to provide an impetus to dig a little further and rediscover what has been lost.

And to remind you, here are the four themes of the book:

1. Christianity has been thoroughly infiltrated by Greek philosophy, particularly the ideas of Plato, resulting in a dualism that has negatively affected every area of doctrine and practice.
2. A return to the Jewish roots of the faith can benefit the Church, not only through an understanding of the equal validity of both the physical and the spiritual, but also through rediscovering Hebraic elements that were banished by the early Church.
3. The only way the Church can attain the One New Man of Ephesians 2 is by Jew and Gentile respecting each other's perspective and striving for a balance between the two.
4. Christians must learn to flex their faith muscles, switch on their brain and get real with God. A reasonable faith should be our goal.

The Christian Church is hungry for revival. We look at real revivals in the past, such as with the Wesley brothers and the Welsh revival of 1905 and we hanker after them, because we can see what effect they had on not just the Church, but on society too. We study past revivals, we read books and create formulae, we go to conferences about revival and many are willing to jump on a plane to visit the latest "fire from heaven". Everything is man-centred because that is the way we are these days. Humanism and New Age techniques have crept into the Church and we believe that we can truly control the heavenlies, that we can "conjure up" the Holy Spirit at will, that revival is just a whisper away as long as we . . .

As long as we . . . what? That's the point, it isn't all about us. There is no magic formula to second guess God and His sovereign purposes. But there is a principle that is totally biblical and has been either ignored by the Church, broken by the Church or manipulated by the Church.

"My days are like the evening shadow;
I wither away like grass.
But you, O LORD, sit enthroned forever;
your renown endures through all generations.
You will arise and have compassion on Zion,
for it is time to show favour to her;
the appointed time has come.
For her stones are dear to your servants;
her very dust moves them to pity.
The nations will fear the name of the LORD,
all the kings of the earth will revere your glory.
For the LORD will rebuild Zion
and appear in his glory.
He will respond to the prayer of the destitute;
he will not despise their plea.

Let this be written for a future generation,
that a people not yet created may praise the LORD :
'The LORD looked down from his sanctuary on high,
from heaven he viewed the earth,
to hear the groans of the prisoners
and release those condemned to death.'"
(Psalm 102:11–20)

A time has been coming when the Jew will not be marginalised, misunderstood or maligned (and this is just the "m"s), but a supernatural veil will be lifted from Jewish people and Jesus will be revealed to them and another veil will be lifted from the Church, and there will be the *appointed time to show favour on Zion.* Read Romans 11, for the full script and explanation. This needs a change in heart, a true repentant attitude by Gentile Christians. And it's our best chance of real, authentic revival!

It's not a clever formula, you can't fool God. Those who promote the "prosperity gospel" promote the idea of giving to God purely to get a blessing in return (whether 10-fold, 100-fold or 1000-fold). God is not a divine lottery of blessings. A change in heart attitude is needed first and foremost and the rest is up to God.

> *"So the name of the* Lord *will be declared in Zion*
> *and his praise in Jerusalem*
> *when the peoples and the kingdoms*
> *assemble to worship the* Lord*."*
> (Psalm 102:21–22)

For the peoples and kingdoms to assemble together to worship the Lord is surely the hallmark of revival. To do this, the name of the Lord will be declared by Jewish people, in Jerusalem, in Israel. The Jewish people are very possibly the keys to revival, in the context of a partnership with Gentiles in the Body of Christ, as our *One New Man*. Meditate on this, particularly in the context of this book and let it seep into your spirit.

Back to the title of this book, *How the Church lost The Way*. We read about the early Church, when it was known as The Way, in Acts 24. Here Paul makes a declaration:

> *"However, I admit that I worship the God of our fathers as a follower of*
> *the Way, which they call a sect. I believe everything that agrees with the*
> *Law and that is written in the Prophets, and I have the same hope in God*
> *as these men, that there will be a resurrection of both the righteous and*
> *the wicked."*
> (Acts 24:14–15)

Here Paul has been accused of creating a sect, yet he affirms that this faith in Jesus is simply a natural progression of the faith of his fathers, the Jews of the Old Testament. This was all it was meant to be, the faith as proclaimed by the words of the Bible, not seen as two different stories, the Old and the New Testament, but as a seamless whole, one story, the story of God and His people.

How the Church lost The Way . . . *and how it can find it again.* Yes, we can find it again, we can return to that pure faith of the Scriptures. We just need to be willing to look for it.

And so I end my story. There is much here that is probably new to you. What I am proposing is not a new revelation or secret doctrine uncovered, it is a sincere desire for the Church to return to its *true* Jewish roots so that the *One New Man* can arise and bless the world.

If I were asked to summarise the whole thrust of my argument in this book, it would be for every sincere Christian *to take personal responsibility.* Don't get blown hither and thither by every new "revelation" that passes by, but instead get into the Scriptures with fellow spiritual sojourners. Be Bereans and test everything, discuss everything and move forwards anchored in the certainties of the revealed Word of God. Examine the Bible through the eyes and experiences of the early Jewish believers, rather than the contact lens of Greek philosophy and re-evaluate your image of God and your attitude to worship and fellowship.

This is not a licence to go it alone, to leave your church or fellowship and stop listening to your vicar, pastor or minister. It is simply an encouragement to go deeper in your faith, using your God-given gifts alongside others to build up the Body of Christ, rather than as a casual observer. And, at every possible opportunity pray to God to light up your path and lead you into all truth. There are exciting times ahead for those who will pick up this gauntlet and run with it.

If this works for you, if it makes sense and draws you closer to God and helps you in your witness to the world, then let's move forward together. If any or all of what I have said does not sit comfortably with you then just take what you can and stay on the path you are already on. Perhaps our paths will cross in the future? We are still brothers and sisters in the Lord, we still work out our salvation with fear and trembling, none of that changes.

> *"God is spirit, and his worshipers must worship in spirit and in truth."*
> (John 4:24)

Appendix 1: Recommended Reading

As I have already said, this is a huge subject and there's a lot of reading material around, though much of it not easily accessible for non-academics like you and I. Here are a few books that I think you will find useful, arranged by chapter of this book.

A Tale of Two Summits – Part 1
The Bible, The Acts of the Apostles, Dr Luke AD 70 (approx.).

God's Extended "Gap Year"
Introducing Philosophy – a graphic guide to the history of thinking, Robinson & Groves, Icon Books, 2007.

Beware Greeks Bearing Gifts
A History of Biblical Interpretation: Ancient Period v. 1, Hauser & Watson, Eerdmans, 2003.

A Tale of Two Summits – Part 2
Backgrounds of Early Christianity, Everett Ferguson, Eerdmans, 2003.

Things Ain't What They Seem
Pagan Christianity, Frank Viola and George Barna, Tyndale House, 2008.

The Kosher Cavalry Arrives
Our Father Abraham: Jewish Roots of the Christian Faith, Marvin R. Wilson, Eerdmans, 1989.

Thus Sayeth the Lord . . . Allegedly!
Homecoming – Our Return to Biblical Roots, Chuck & Karen
Cohen, Sovereign World, 2008.

Every Day with Yeshua, Every Year with God
The Gospel in the Feasts of Israel, Victor Buksbazen, Christian
    Literature Crusade, 1954.

There's No Place Like Home
When a Jew Celebrates, Gersh & Weihs, Behrman House
    Publishing, 1971.

Our Father God
The Jewish Approach to God, Rabbi Neil Gillman, Jewish Lights
    Publishing, 2003.

Redoing Religion
The Jewish Holidays, Michael Strassfeld, Collins, 1993.

God's Language Unravelled
Listening to the Language of the Bible, Tverberg & Okkema,
    En-Gedi Resource Center, 2006.

One New Man Revisited
One New Man, Reuven Doron, Embrace Israel Ministries, 1999.
The Last Lap, Sid Roth, M V Press, 2001.

The People of Many Names
The People of Many Names, Steve Maltz, Authentic Media, 2005.

Finding One New Home
The Messianic Church Arising!, Dr Robert D. Heidler, Glory of
    Zion, 2006.

Appendix 2: Now Why Don't You . . . ?

At the current time four of my books are still available for purchase, either through Amazon, Christian bookshops or directly from www.saffronplanet.net

The Land of Many Names: *Towards a Christian understanding of the Middle East conflict*
This book has been generally accepted in the UK as the most balanced, well-reasoned and clear explanation of the position taken by those Christians who believe that God still has a purpose for Israel today.

> *"This book lives up to the blurb in its style – lively, entertaining and provocative – it gives a well-researched and popular account of Israel's history from the days of Abram to Sharon . . . Addictive, dented some of my convictions and made me think hard."*
> Tony Sargent, Principal of International Christian College, Glasgow

The People of Many Names: *Towards a clearer understanding of the miracle of the Jewish people*
This book pulls no punches in providing an insight into God's plan for the Jew, Christian anti-semitism and includes practical suggestions for reconciliation within the Body of Messiah.

> *"I think it's brilliant, inspired, a great read, of interest to both Jews and Christians, a breath of fresh air – and timely! What more can I say!"*
> Julia Fisher, writer and broadcaster.

Jesus, the Man of Many Names: *A Fresh Understanding from the dawn of time to the End of Days*
Are you prepared for a new book about Jesus that does offer fresh insights without boasting new revelations? Drawing on sources from the Jewish world, ancient and modern, the author will take you on an exhilarating, lively and entertaining exploration of the life and times of the Jewish Messiah.

> *"Steve Maltz has a gift for combining pacy writing with crystal-clear distillation of his own careful study of scholarly resources and a firm grip on the Gospel. The result is a fascinating new landscape of insight"*
> David Andrew, editor *Sword* Magazine

The Truth Is Out There: *The Ultimate World Conspiracy.*
Who really is pulling the strings?
Is history just a random sequence of events, or are there secret manipulations? What makes us tick? How did the World as we see it come to be? Read this book if you are prepared to be challenged.

> *"Steve Maltz has a rare gift of being able to communicate complex ideas in a way that leaves you thinking that you have read the work of a genius but can still follow his argument clearly. A brilliant read for an evangelist to engage with a sceptic or to give as a gift for 'food for thought'"*
> Tim Leffler, The GoodBookstall.org.uk